Theology For the Charismatic Church

David Young

CROWN TRUST BOOKS
Woodbridge, VA

Introduction

Copyright © 2023 by David Young. All rights reserved.

Dyoung7707@outlook.com

Unless otherwise indicated, all Scripture is from the New International Version.

The Holy Bible, New International Version NIV Copyright © 1973, 1978, 1984, 2011 by Biblica, Inc. Used by permission. All rights reserved worldwide.

ESV

The ESV Bible (*The Holy Bible, English Standard Version*). ESV Text Edition: 2016. Copyright © 2001 by Crossway, a publishing ministry of Good News Publishers. The ESV text has been reproduced in cooperation with and by permission of Good News Publishers.

NASB

New American Standard Bible, Copyright © 1960, 1971, 1977, 1995, 2020 by the Lockman Foundation. All rights reserved.

Phillips

The New Testament in Modern English by J.B. Phillips copyright © 1960, 1972 J. B. Phillips. Administered by the Archbishops' Council of the Church of England. Used by permission.

Table of Contents

INTRODUCTION..1
CHAPTER 1 WHAT IT MEANS TO BE CHARISMATIC 4
- Baptism in the Spirit 5
- Hungering after God... 7
- A Strong Belief in the Supernatural............................ 8
- A Sense of Expectancy and Participation 9
- Summary 11

CHAPTER 2 SPIRIT BAPTISM 13
- The New Birth.. 14
- New Birth and Spirit Baptism 16
- A Reformed View: Walter Kaiser 18
- A Catholic Perspective: Ralph Del Colle 19
- A Pentecostal Perspective: Stanley M. Horton 20
- A Charismatic Perspective: Larry Hart 22
- You Will Receive Power 23
- The Holy Spirit and the Human Spirit 29
- The Release of the Spirit.. 34
- Tares Among the Wheat 34
- Summary 35

CHAPTER 3 SPIRITUAL GIFTS 37
- What Are Spiritual Gifts? 37
- Gift Groups 39
- Prophetic Gifts... 39
- Power Gifts 40
- Teaching and Preaching 41
- Serving Gifts 42
- Desiring and Acquiring Spiritual Gifts 43
- Discovering the Spirit and His Gifts 47
- Dreams, Visions, and Revelations............................ 50
- Summary 52

Introduction

CHAPTER 4 SUPERNATURAL GIFTS ARE FOR TODAY 53
- CESSATIONISM 53
- MIDDLE OF THE ROAD 57
- PENTECOSTAL, CHARISMATIC, AND THIRD WAVE 59
- APOSTLES AND PROPHETS 64
- WORDS OF CAUTION ABOUT APOSTLES AND PROPHETS 67
- SUMMARY 72

CHAPTER 5 THE POWER OF FAITH 74
- LIMITATIONS ON FAITH 79
- THE SUPERNATURAL ASPECT OF FAITH 81
- FAITH AS A LIFESTYLE 83
- SUMMARY 85

CHAPTER 6 SPIRIT AND SCRIPTURE 87
- THE BIBLE AS HISTORY 88
- THE BIBLE AS A LEGAL TEXT 90
- THE BIBLE AS A SPIRITUAL TEXT 91
- SENSUS PLENIOR: THE SPIRITUAL MEANING OF THE TEXT 93
- THEOLOGICAL NARRATIVE 95
- THE SPIRITUALITY OF THE INTERPRETER 99
- SUMMARY 102

CHAPTER 7 CHARISMATIC SPIRITUALITY 104
- SPIRITUAL AWARENESS AND UNDERSTANDING 106
- THE MIND OF CHRIST 109
- SPIRITUALITY AND HOLINESS 111
- WALKING IN POWER 117
- SUMMARY 119

CHAPTER 8 PARTICIPATION WITH CHRIST 120
- PARTICIPATION IN THE OLD TESTAMENT 120
- PARTICIPATION IN THE NEW TESTAMENT 121
- MINISTRY IN CONTEXT 123
- SUMMARY 125

CHAPTER 9 THE ROLE OF THE CHARISMATIC CHURCH 127
- THE ROLE OF THE CHURCH IN SPIRITUAL FORMATION 128

The Church as a House of Prayer 131
Praying in Tongues... 134
The Church's Role in Spiritual Gifts 136
Promoting Holiness 138
The Church as a Place of Healing 141
Summary 144

CHAPTER 10 DEMONS AND SPIRITUAL WARFARE 146

The Origin of Satan and Demons 147
Kingdoms in Conflict 151
Demonic Attacks on Believers 157
Casting Out Demons 162
Suggestions for Delivering People from Demons . 164
Summary 166

Introduction

Introduction

There are two distinctive features of this book. First, it is written from a Charismatic perspective. There are many books written from a Pentecostal perspective that include Charismatic theology as well, but this book is primarily Charismatic in perspective. There are many similarities between Pentecostal theology and Charismatic theology, but there are also significant differences. Those issues are explored in *Chapter 1, What Does It Mean to Be Charismatic?* The second distinctive feature is that it is addressed to the Charismatic church. Most books are written for individuals, but the aim of this book is to help Spirit-filled people learn to live together in community with others.

Chapters 2 through 5 deal with Spirit baptism, spiritual gifts, and works of faith. *Chapter 2, Spirit Baptism*, discusses what is perhaps the most controversial aspect of Charismatic faith and the main area that distinguishes Charismatics from Pentecostals. While Charismatics have much in common with Pentecostals, Charismatics assert that the fullness of the Spirit is received at the moment of salvation. Participating with Christ through the gifts and ministries of the Spirit is immediately available to all believers from the moment of salvation, but we may have (and should have) additional experiences that further equip us for ministry. Those additional experiences may be referred to as baptism(s) or fillings with the Spirit. We agree with Larry Hart, who finds that Spirit baptism is a descriptive phrase with many meanings; the meanings can include all aspects of the Spirit's work in and through the believer.[1] *Chapter 3, Spiritual Gifts*, is an introduction to spiritual gifts. I chose not to give a definition for each gift because I take the position that the gifts listed in the Bible are examples and not an exhaustive list. *Chapter 4, Supernatural Gifts Are for Today*, is an apologia for the gifts and responds to those who say that the supernatural gifts, sometimes called sign gifts, ceased at the end of the first century. *Chapter 5, The Power of Faith*, is closely related to spiritual gifts but is broader in that it seeks to demonstrate how faith, in general, can "move mountains," which is a metaphor for doing that which is humanly impossible. Chapter 5 also discusses the limitations of faith: i.e., works of faith are limited to the sovereign will of God.

Chapter 6, Spirit and Scripture, discusses the typical way in which many Charismatics read and interpret biblical narratives. Charismatics take a participatory stance with the Scriptures. We do not read the Bible mainly as the history of early biblical times but rather to hear God speak to us today as he invites us to participate in his activities. *Chapter 7, Charismatic Spirituality*, explores what is commonly referred to as spiritual formation. The Charismatic faith and worldview uniquely posture Charismatics for spiritual formation in areas such as having the mind of Christ, discerning of spirits, and holiness. *Chapter 8, Participation with Christ*, highlights a main theme of Charismatic theology; we, as Spirit-filled believers, are called and empowered by the Spirit to participate in his work. *Chapter 9, The Role of the Charismatic Church*, addresses the unique features of a body of believers who pursue participation in the Spirit. This chapter highlights the role of the church in helping believers discover, acquire, and develop their spiritual gifts.

Chapter 10, Demons and Spiritual Warfare, was deliberately placed at the end because it incorporates material from throughout the book and also because I do not want to make demons the centerpiece of the book. As important as spiritual warfare is, it should not be the center, or most important element, of theology. However, the New Testament teaches that we are involved in spiritual warfare on a regular basis—probably more so than we recognize. Many of Jesus' healing miracles involved deliverance from demonism. We cannot be effective in our

Introduction

own personal lives or in ministry unless we recognize the battle between the kingdom of God and the kingdom of darkness.

Chapter 1
What It Means to Be Charismatic

We must begin this project by defining what we mean by the term *Charismatic*. In this book, I define a Charismatic as a Christian who has a deep awareness of the Holy Spirit's presence and who believes that the Holy Spirit continues to work with supernatural manifestations (supernatural gifts of the Spirit) through Christians today. This awareness of the Spirit's presence results in a supernatural worldview and an expectancy that God desires to be at work in the church in much the same way that he did in the Book of Acts. We take the view that Baptism in the Spirit occurs at salvation and may or may not be accompanied by a spiritual gift; some people will, of course, disagree.[2] The Greek word *charisma* simply means gift, and it comes from the root word *charis*, which means grace. When we put the concepts together, as occurs in 1 Corinthians 12 and 14, they imply gifts of grace. Another word for grace is *pneumatikos*, which means spirituals or spiritual things (1 Cor. 12 and 14). From that background, we have formed the English word *charismatic* to describe someone who emphasizes the supernatural work of God, especially spiritual gifts.

Historically, the term *Charismatic* can be applied to a movement that grew out of Pentecostalism.[3] The modern Pentecostal movement began with revival experiences nearly simultaneously at a Bible college in Topeka, Kansas (1901) and also at a revival at a small church on Azusa Street in Los Angeles (1906). This first wave of the Spirit was followed by a second wave, starting in the early 1960s. This second wave involved people from many different denominations, including Catholic, Anglican, Methodist, and others. Studies show that by the mid-1960s, people in "virtually every Protestant tradition" were receiving this spiritual experience.[4] People involved in this second wave were generally known as Charismatics because while they shared the Pentecostal emphasis on the Holy Spirit, many of them did not accept the classical Pentecostal doctrine that Spirit baptism is a second work of grace, subsequent to salvation, and is always accompanied by speaking in other tongues. Charismatics freely use the term *Baptism in the Spirit*, but they may explain it in different ways. Some see it as an awakening of the believer to the Spirit's presence. Others may explain it as a stirring up of the Spirit within. Others say that a person may have multiple baptisms or fillings with the Spirit in addition to the baptism into the body of Christ that occurs at salvation.

This book will take the position that to be Charismatic relates to one's experience with the Holy Spirit, which results in a deeper understanding of the Spirit's work in our contemporary times. This deeper understanding is more experiential than cognitive. Charismatic is not a doctrine per se, but it normally results in a strong belief and expectation that the Spirit wants to work in and through Christian believers today in much the same way that he did in biblical times. We find that there are certain characteristics of the Spirit-filled life that mark one as being Charismatic. To that end, we are offering four marks of the Charismatic life and church. These marks are not exclusive to those who identify as Charismatic. Many people are charismatic (small c) in practice but do not identify with a particular Charismatic church or movement.

Baptism in the Spirit

Baptism in the Holy Spirit may be the first concept that comes to mind when one speaks of Charismatic or Pentecostal.[5] Although Charismatics tend to use the term *baptized in the Spirit* more frequently, the term *filled with the Spirit* is also used, sometimes interchangeably.

Reformed evangelicals hold that being baptized in the Spirit properly refers to the salvation experience when the new believer is baptized into the body of Christ (1 Cor. 12:13) and filled with the Spirit refers to subsequent experiences of being filled with the Spirit's power (Eph. 5:18). We will address these differences more in Chapter 2, but at this point, we simply want to look at the outcome of the experience without getting into the doctrinal aspects.

In Jesus' instructions to his disciples, which Luke repeated in Acts 1, we find him saying: "But you will receive power when the Holy Spirit comes on you, and you will be my witnesses in Jerusalem, and in all Judea and Samaria, and to the ends of the earth" (Acts 1:8). It is this promise of power that inspires Charismatics to seek a more robust relationship with the Holy Spirit than is commonly found among many Christians. Nearly all evangelicals acknowledge that one can be a Christian and yet lack the kind of power that Luke is referring to. The debate over how and when that power comes to the believer will wait until a later chapter, but we acknowledge here that having the power to serve God and live victoriously is at the heart of what it means to be Charismatic. As we look at the additional marks stated below—such as a strong belief in the supernatural and a sense of expectancy—we see a common thread of how the Spirit transforms and empowers the believer to participate in the miraculous work of God.

Charismatics share much in common with Pentecostals, but we also have some differences. For Charismatics, Spirit baptism is more of an individual experience than a doctrine. The power of the Spirit may be received in many different ways and at different stages in our journey. Larry Hart writes: "The gift of the Holy Spirit is the culmination of Christian initiation [salvation], however experienced. Our pilgrimages are about as diverse as our personalities."[6] Glossolalia (speaking in tongues) is a gift of the Spirit and is accepted and sought after the same as any other gift, not more or less. Some will argue that tongues as a sign are different than tongues as a gift, and everyone may have the sign (or prayer language) even if they don't have the gift, but most Charismatics do not believe that speaking in tongues is essential to Spirit baptism. Speaking in tongues is less of an issue outside the United States than it is among American Christians. One knowledgeable source reported that less than half of the Brazilian Pentecostals speak in tongues, but the majority relate to divine healing as a prominent attribute of their faith.[7]

If you claim to be Charismatic, you are in good company. According to a 1998 *Newsweek* poll, 47 percent of the Christians surveyed said they had "personally experienced the Holy Spirit."[8] Other sources report that nearly 30 percent of Christians worldwide (523 million) identify as Pentecostal or Charismatic,[9] with a reported "33 million Pentecostals and Charismatics in India."[10] In the West, we tend to think of all of Africa as being predominately Muslim, but in South Africa, more than half the people are Pentecostal.[11]

Hungering after God

One of the key marks of Charismatic Christianity is a hungering after God. To hunger after God is not unique to any denomination or group of Christians, but it is a mark of a Spirit-filled Christian and, therefore, of being Charismatic. So what I am proposing is that one of the outcomes of being baptized in the Spirit is that he gives us the gift of desiring him more. This desire is not merely a human preference or a psychological phenomenon, but it is a Spirit-initiated craving that seeks more of God and his divine presence. It is possible to have the Spirit, at least within the meaning of Romans 8:9 and yet not have this inner craving for more. Not all Christians live under the Spirit's influence such that they are mindful of his presence on a daily basis. This mind that seeks after God on is the result of two factors. First, it is the work of the Spirit himself and flows from conversion. Second, the hunger and the seeking after God continue and grow by the conscious decision of the Christian to desire God and to place knowing him as one of their highest priorities in life. A Charismatic is one who fans the flames of God's Spirit and continuously surrenders himself or herself to God. Paul warned that we should not "quench the Spirit" (1

Thess. 5:19). If the Spirit can be quenched, he can also be encouraged and ignited through our surrender to him.

God is at work in all people, including non-Christians and those of other faiths.[12] The Spirit draws people to Christ and enables them to have saving faith. "No one can come to me unless the Father who sent me draws them" (Jn. 6:44). God plants within the human spirit a desire to be in relationship with him, and he enables us to respond to the work of the Spirit. Our response to the drawing of the Spirit determines whether God's work is effective in our lives.[13] Those who accept Christ as Savior do so because God has enabled them to believe unto salvation. The seeking after God that we have described as a mark of the Charismatic life is an outgrowth of the work of the Spirit that began with the Spirit's drawing and continued and increased in the new birth experience. We must never lose sight, however, that any desire we have for God is, first of all, a gift from God. The Holy Spirit works within the human spirit to restore the image of God that was tarnished during the fall. The Spirit molds us in God's image through the fruit of the Spirit. As the fruit of the Spirit grows, it removes and replaces the fruit and desires of the human flesh. As we become more like Christ, our desire for him increases, as does our disdain for the sinfulness of the old world. The light within us no longer desires the darkness of the old life. We want more and more of God and to experience his Spirit in our lives.

A Strong Belief in the Supernatural

A belief in miracles and the supernatural was quite common throughout the world until the Enlightenment era, which began in the early seventeenth century. The Enlightenment philosophers proposed that everything that happens and everything that exists can be explained by science; everything else is mere superstition. Enlightenment thinking and its associated anti-supernatural bias continues to control academia, including many seminaries and divinity schools. Rudolph Bultmann is considered by many to be the most influential theologian of the twentieth century, and his hermeneutical methods have influenced nearly every Bible commentary, including those written by evangelicals. Bultmann argued that the biblical concept of miracles must be considered "myths" because miracles contradict the laws of nature as determined by modern science. Therefore, the idea of miracles is no longer tenable."[14] Bultmann further opines that even if Jesus and Paul believed in such myths, we are not required to do so.

In contrast, Charismatics firmly hold that God is sovereign over science. God established the so-called laws of science, and God can make exceptions. God is not limited by the laws he established. The early Pentecostals were mostly uneducated working-class men and women.[15] By the time the Charismatic movements began in the 1960s, many educated people were drawn into them. Today's Charismatics include men and women with graduate degrees and high academic honors from the most acclaimed schools in the world. And yet, a distinguishing mark of Charismatic faith is an ardent belief in the supernatural. Within this, we would include miracles, as well as belief in a supernatural world that includes God, angels, a personal devil, and demons. The Charismatic views all of life with this supernatural worldview. Miracles happen! Charismatics are firm in their belief that the supernatural world is just as real as the material world and more powerful.

A Sense of Expectancy and Participation

Charismatics expect the Spirit to work in their midst in much the same way that he did in the early church and as recorded in the Book of Acts. James Smith describes this as a "radical openness to God."[16] The term *radical openness* aptly describes the Charismatic worldview in which all things are possible, and nothing should be rejected a priori. Charismatic theology assumes that everything that happened in the New Testament could happen today. The Charismatic Christian will often read the Bible and see themselves in the biblical story. We do not believe that we live in a different dispensation of time when those things are no longer possible. We could spend a lot of time arguing about cessationism versus continuance, but at this point, we are simply describing the marks of a Charismatic—we will defend this more in Chapter 4. As with the other marks, we are not claiming this expectancy is unique to Charismatics. As we will discuss further in chapter 6, narrative theology is gaining in prominence, and it presents the concept that we are invited to participate in the biblical story. The modern reader sees the Bible as a history book; the Charismatic reads it as God's living Word speaking afresh to every generation. The Charismatic participates in the biblical story.

Not only does the Charismatic expect God to act in similar ways today as he did in the first century, but they also take Joel's prophecy concerning the last days seriously.

> In the last days, God says, I will pour out my Spirit on all people. Your sons and daughters will prophesy, your young men will see visions, your old men will dream dreams. Even on my servants, both men and women, I will pour out my Spirit in those days, and they will prophesy. Acts 2:17–18

The Charismatic will argue that when Peter preached, saying, "These are the last days, and this is what Joel was speaking of," we are still living in those last days, which began at Pentecost and will continue until the return of Christ. The *last days* do not end prior to his return. Joel's prophecy indicates that the outpouring of the Spirit is not for a select few—such as ministers and priests—but for all God's people: men and women, young and old. Joel's prophecy especially emphasizes verbal and revelational gifts. While it does not exclude healing and other gifts of a material nature, they are not specifically mentioned. The Book of Acts confirms that while physical miracles such as healing did occur among people of all statuses (not just the apostles), occurrences of prophetic utterances were more common than other miracles. Charismatics today value inspired speech, as did the early church.

What it Means to Be Charismatic

Charismatics not only expect God to perform miracles, but we also expect to participate in God's work. The whole purpose of spiritual gifts is not for personal enjoyment or betterment but so we can participate with God in his work. We are not mere spectators who observe what God is doing, nor are we historians discovering what God did in the past, but we are called and empowered to actively participate in the work of God. This will be explored more in Chapter eight.

Summary

This chapter describes what we mean by the term *Charismatic*. Craig Keener prefers the term *Spirit-filled*, and he argues that if we include everyone who believes in the fullness of the Spirit's power, including supernatural gifts, the majority of Christians worldwide fit into this category.[17] There are four key attributes of what it means to be Charismatic—or one could as easily use the term *pneumatic*. First, Charismatic people place special emphasis on the indwelling of the Spirit, which they may refer to as *Baptism in the Spirit* or *filled with the Spirit*. Second, Charismatic people characteristically have a strong desire or hungering for more of God's presence in their lives. Third, Charismatics have a worldview that includes a strong belief in the supernatural presence of God and his activities in the world today. This worldview assumes that God is not limited to the laws of nature or to scientific methods of inquiry. Fourth, Charismatics not only acknowledge that God has acted supernaturally in the past, but they also expect God to continue operating supernaturally in modern times. Along with this sense of expectancy concerning what God might do, Charismatics expect to participate in what God is doing. Participation is not limited to those called or ordained to professional ministry; all believers are filled with the Spirit and invited by God to participate in his work.

According to polls conducted by George Gallup and the Pew Foundation, nearly one-third of the people in Europe and America have Charismatic beliefs, and in some other countries, the number is nearly two-thirds.[18] The purpose of this book is to provide information and encouragement to Spirit-filled believers regardless of their denominational identity.

Chapter 2
Spirit Baptism

> Jesus answered, "Very truly I tell you, no one can enter the kingdom of God unless they are born of water and the Spirit. Flesh gives birth to flesh, but the Spirit gives birth to spirit. You should not be surprised at my saying, 'You must be born again.' The wind blows wherever it pleases. You hear its sound, but you cannot tell where it comes from or where it is going. So it is with everyone born of the Spirit." John 3:5–8

Classical Pentecostal theology teaches that Spirit baptism is a separate experience that occurs after the new birth and is evidenced by speaking in tongues.[19] Many contemporary Pentecostals no longer hold to the twin doctrines of "subsequence" and "initial evidence," and they see Spirit baptism as something that grows out of and continues the new birth experience.[20] Frank Macchia, a Pentecostal scholar, argues that subsequence and initial evidence are no longer important issues among most Pentecostals,[21] and some researchers conclude that only about 30 percent of those who attend Pentecostal churches speak in tongues.[22] Of course, there are other Pentecostals who strongly disagree with these findings and argue that one is not truly Pentecostal without the evidence of speaking in tongues.[23] Some Charismatics hold the classical Pentecostal position, but most do not.[24] It is not the intent of this book to argue for one position or another, but we will take the view that to be born again is to be born of the Spirit. At the same time, and on many subsequent occasions, an individual can and should receive additional outpourings, baptisms, and fillings of the Spirit that enable the believer to participate in the supernatural Spirit-filled life.

The New Birth

No one can see the kingdom of God (Jn. 3:3) or enter the kingdom (Jn. 3:5) unless they are born of the Spirit. During the new birth, the human spirit becomes regenerated with new spiritual perceptions. The kingdom of God is in our midst, but we cannot see it or have an awareness of it unless our spiritual eyes are opened. After Jesus' resurrection, he walked along the road to Emmaus with two disciples. At first, the two men didn't recognize Jesus. However, after he broke bread with them, he opened their spiritual eyes so they could recognize him (Lk. 24:31–32). The breaking of bread is similar to that memorialized in communion or Eucharist, and as demonstrated on the Emmaus Road, it is more than symbolic—it is real, and it is effective.

The new birth prepares the way for an awakening experience that both transforms and empowers. The new birth (salvation) allows the Holy Spirit to come into the believer's life so that he (the Spirit) can do his work, but not every believer grows spiritually so that the awakening, empowering, and transformation come to maturity. Some churches believe that sanctification and empowerment through baptism in the Spirit must always come as separate experiences subsequent to salvation, but the apostles expected sanctification and empowerment to begin immediately and to be the natural outflow of the new birth. Peter expected this to happen when he wrote, "Repent and be baptized, every one of you, in the name of Jesus Christ for the forgiveness of your sins, and you will receive the gift of the Holy Spirit" (Acts 2:38). But this does not always occur. When Paul questioned the people from Ephesus, he asked them, "Did you receive the Holy Spirit when you believed?" They answered, "No, we have not even heard that there is a Holy Spirit" (Acts 19:2). Some Bible scholars argue that these men were not saved, and that is why they had not received the Spirit.[25] However, the fact that they were described as disciples who believed is consistent with how the apostles described Christians throughout the New Testament.

The late James D. G. Dunn is no doubt correct when he says that in Paul's mind, there could be no genuine conversion without a display of the Spirit's power.[26] Likewise, F. F. Bruce states, "Receiving the Spirit, then with the experience of his power, is for Paul an essential element in Christian initiation. Indeed, he cannot envisage any true believer who has not received the Spirit or experienced his power."[27] The apostles questioned the baptismal experience of the men from Ephesus (Acts 19:6) because they had not experienced the Spirit in any recognizable way. Paul then laid hands on the men, and they received the Spirit (Acts 19:6). Commentators debate why the men from Ephesus acknowledged Jesus as savior: they had been baptized in water, but they had not experienced the Spirit. Despite centuries of debate, that question has not been answered, and the apostles did not find it necessary to offer an explanation. As with the Samaritan believers (Acts 8:14–17), all we know for sure is that the apostles expected people to receive the Spirit at the time of conversion.

The Great Awakening (eighteenth century) involved the work of John Wesley, Jonathan Edwards, and George Whitefield. Although they differed in some areas of doctrine (Wesley was Arminian, and Edwards and Whitefield were Calvinists), they agreed on one important principle: when people are genuinely saved, they should have an experience with the Holy Spirit. The experience need not be a dramatic outwardly observable experience, but in most cases, it would be an inner experience observable only to the person. This was unfamiliar teaching to most of the people of that time. Wesley, Whitefield, and Edwards were shunned by many members of the clergy for preaching that new believers should experience the confirmation of the Spirit.

There are three aspects of salvation: justification, regeneration, and sanctification. Justification means that God declares the sinner to be no longer guilty. Justification is not an experience; it is a change in status. Regeneration, however, means that something has been made new. Regeneration requires the work of the Spirit to change the heart of the believer. Jesus said, "Truly I tell you, unless you change and become like little children, you will never enter the kingdom of heaven" (Matt. 18:3). Justification does not occur without regeneration—a change in the person. This is what it means to be born of the Spirit; Spirit gives birth to spirit. The third aspect of salvation is sanctification; this is a gradual process of spiritual growth. The New Testament always assumes that justification (change of status), regeneration (change of heart), and sanctification (gradual growth) always start at the same time and progress according to God's work in our lives. The idea that a person could receive justification but not have any spiritual experience is foreign to the New Testament.

New Birth and Spirit Baptism

> For John baptized with water, but in a few days, you will be baptized with the Holy Spirit. Acts 1:5

> But you will receive power when the Holy Spirit comes on you; and you will be my witnesses in Jerusalem, and in all Judea and Samaria, and to the ends of the earth. Acts 1:8

The Pentecostal outpouring that began in the early part of the twentieth century (1901 in Topeka, KS, and 1906 in Los Angeles) brought a fresh new emphasis on Spirit baptism. Along with this new emphasis came vigorous discussions of the related theological doctrines. The mainstream Pentecostal denominations—principally the Assemblies of God and the Church of God (Cleveland, TN)—formalized the twin doctrines of subsequence and evidence. Subsequence means that the baptism in the Spirit is a distinct experience that occurs after regeneration. Evidence means that

Spirit Baptism

baptism in the Spirit is *always* accompanied by glossolalia (speaking in tongues). The reason for the new emphasis on Spirit baptism is that many believers had never experienced the power of the Spirit that Jesus said would come upon those who believed. The same is true of the Charismatic renewal that began in the mid–twentieth century (the 1960s). Christian believers were hungry for the Spirit's power. A move of the Spirit began—probably in California, according to church historians—and swept across the country and internationally.[28] The new movement was labeled Charismatic to distinguish it from Pentecostalism. Although Pentecostals and Charismatics share much in common, many charismatics wanted to remain in their traditional mainline churches. They saw themselves as Charismatic (or Spirit-filled) Methodists, Baptists, Catholics, and Episcopalians—they did not want to leave their denominations and join a Pentecostal church. The other difference between Pentecostals and the new Charismatics is that Charismatics embrace the fullness of the Spirit, but most of them do not embrace the Pentecostal doctrines of subsequence and initial evidence. Many, but not all, Charismatics speak in tongues, but they did not then (nor do they now) emphasize speaking in tongues as the sign of the baptism in the Spirit. If there must be a sign of the Spirit's presence, it is his power.

Recent discussions concerning new birth and Spirit baptism have produced a consensus that Luke and Paul refer to Spirit baptism from different perspectives. Luke writes from the perspective of what happens after salvation—the Spirit provides power for service. Paul uses the same words to emphasize what happens at the moment of salvation—the new believer is baptized into the body of Christ. Biblical interpretation in past centuries assumed that since the Holy Spirit inspired the biblical writers, they all wrote from the same perspective and used the same lexicon. Recent scholarship tends to emphasize the diversity of the human authors as they wrote under the inspiration of the Spirit.[29] We find that the human authors retained their own unique vocabularies and Spirit-inspired interests in what they wanted to write. The current thinking is that the center of Luke's theology is found in the Book of Acts, and the center of Paul's theology is found in Romans. Each writer reports on the work of the Holy Spirit from a different perspective, and neither view is complete without the other.[30]

In Chad Brand's book *Perspectives on Spirit Baptism: Five Views*, five different authors provided their views of Spirit baptism. I am summarizing four of them here to provide further insight.

A Reformed View: Walter Kaiser

> The Spirit reception is part of Christian initiation [Spirit baptism happens at the new birth].[31]

> The baptism of the Holy Spirit is a distinctive blessing of the new Age in which all believers are made to participate and drink of the Holy Spirit. . . . It continues to be possible for all believers to be filled with the Holy Spirit and empowered for specific tasks at specific times.[32]

In this last statement, Kaiser distinguishes between Baptism and filling. He asserts that Spirit baptism occurs only once, but a person may be filled on many occasions. Kaiser adopts the Reformed position that doctrinal theology must be based on didactic passages rather than narrative. For that reason, Kaiser and others tend to downplay the use of Acts as a basis for theology. The argument is that narrative, such as the book of Acts, is merely a record of what happened; it is not necessarily normative for the church going forward. The Charismatic response to this is that narrative was given for our use as doctrine, not just for historical purposes but for our learning and instruction. "All Scripture is God-breathed and is useful for teaching, rebuking, correcting and training in righteousness" (2 Tim. 3:16).

Spirit Baptism

A Catholic Perspective: Ralph Del Colle

The author acknowledges that the Catholic Church did not talk much about Spirit baptism until 1967, when the Charismatic revival entered the Catholic Church like a mighty wind.[33]

> The story is well-known and need not be rehearsed except to say that at Duquesne University, the University of Notre Dame, and Michigan State University, prayer meetings and later Charismatic communities formed around Catholics newly baptized in the Holy Spirit. From there, it spread to other campuses, parishes, and religious communities, with laypeople, priests, and those in consecrated life taking part. Soon it was a burgeoning movement in the Catholic Church, with bishops and even cardinals actively involved.[34]

Del Colle makes a very important statement when he says, "I highlight 'doctrine' and 'experience' since, for all intents and purposes, they can and ought to be distinguished. That is to say, a Christian may have a Pentecostal-type experience without necessarily assenting to or promoting the classical Pentecostal doctrine."[35] This is an important distinction for all the various views. We share many things in common, but the differences are also significant. Del Colle describes the early Catholic Charismatics in these terms:

> None of the pioneers envisioned a contradiction of Spirit baptism with their Catholic faith. They did not seek an alternative to their Catholic sacramental practice and their experienced forms of prayer and devotion. Rather, and this would prove the rule in the renewal, the new experience of the Holy Spirit complemented and strengthened that faith with members of the movement, often advocating a return to some traditional Catholic devotions.[36]

Theology For the Charismatic Church

What we see in the Charismatic movement across all denominational lines is that Spirit baptism added to people's faith but generally did not draw them away from their denominations or churches. Del Colle finds that to explain Spirit baptism in terms of Catholic theology, it must be situated within the sacraments.[37] Importantly, Catholics rely on the efficacy of the sacraments and do not seek experiential confirmation. Del Colle says that seeking experiential assurances is "alien to the Catholic tradition."[38] Several symposiums were held to explore the implications of the Charismatic movement for Catholic theology. One such symposium held in Germany in 1987 "dealt extensively with the notion of experience, Spirit baptism, and Charismatic renewal. . . . This document is important because it . . . rehabilitates the category of experience for a Catholic theology of grace."[39] Del Colle summarizes by saying that Spirit baptism does not have "doctrinal status" in the Catholic church, which leaves the way open for a variety of interpretations.[40] In general, the Catholic church sees Spirit baptism as a personal experience that involves grace, prayer, and personal communion between the Christian and the Holy Spirit. It does not change the church's view of how God works through the sacraments.

A Pentecostal Perspective: Stanley M. Horton

Horton defends the classical Pentecostal position and frames much of his discussion in terms of the Assemblies of God's "A Statement of Fundamental Truths." In the 1961 revision, paragraphs 7 and 8 are as follows:

> 7. The Baptism in the Holy Ghost. All believers are entitled to and should ardently expect and earnestly seek the promise of the Father, the baptism in the Holy Ghost and fire, according to the command of our Lord Jesus Christ. This was the normal experience of all in the early Christian church. With it comes the enduement of power for life and service, the bestowment of the gifts and their uses in the work

Spirit Baptism

of the ministry (Luke 24:49; Acts 1:4,8:1 Cor. 12:1–31). This experience is distinct from and subsequent to the experience of the new birth (Acts 8:12–17; 10:44–46; 11:114–16; 15:8–9). With the baptism in the Holy Ghost come such experiences as an overflowing fullness of the Spirit (John 7.37–39; Acts 4:8), a deepened reverence for God (Acts 243; Heb. 12:28), an intensified consecration to God and dedication to His work (Acts 2:42), and a more active love Christ, for His Word and for the lost (Mark 15:20).

8. The Initial Physical Evidence of the Baptism in the Holy Ghost. The baptism of believers in the Holy Ghost is witnessed by the initial physical sign of speaking with other tongues as the Spirit of God gives them utterance (Acts 2:4). The speaking in tongues in this instance is the same in essence as the gift of tongues (1 Cor. 12:4–10, 28), but different in purpose and use.

The Assemblies of God's statement outlines what has become known as the "classical Pentecostal" perspective. The two most important attributes are "subsequence" (Spirit baptism is separate and subsequent to the receipt of the Spirit at salvation) and "initial evidence" (speaking in tongues is the initial sign of receiving the Spirit). Horton's discussion does not recognize salvation as a receiving of the Spirit. For example, he discusses several texts which refer to people being spiritual or having spiritual wisdom (Jas. 3:15–17; 1 Thess. 1:5; Jn. 15:26), and he implies that the texts refer to people who have received the Spirit as a second work of grace. The Charismatic and evangelical view is that such texts refer to all Christians who receive the spirit at salvation.

A Charismatic Perspective: Larry Hart

Hart notes that the terms *Spirit baptism* and *filled with the Spirit* are sometimes used interchangeably and sometimes as denoting different experiences. Hart's view acknowledges that the Spirit is received at salvation, and there can be many additional fillings or baptisms (the choice of words is not important to Hart) during a person's life. For Hart and many other Charismatics, Spirit baptism is a metaphor that can include all aspects of the Spirit's work in and through the believer. Hart writes,

> In the Pauline sense of the metaphor, all believers have experienced Spirit baptism. In the Lukan emphasis on the empowering dimension of Spirit baptism, we may not all be "filled with the Spirit"! The traditional view that Spirit baptism, in its regenerational dimension, is what all true believers have in common is correct. But the Pentecostal/Charismatic tradition is also on target in arguing that Luke uses the metaphor (along with at least six others) in an empowering sense.[41]
>
> The metaphors used to describe this experience include:
>
> First, the believers are "baptized in the Holy spirit" (Acts 1:5, 11:16). Second, the Holy Spirit "comes upon" (Acts 1:8; 19:6). Third, the believers are "filled with the Holy Spirit" (Acts 2:4). Fourth, the Holy Spirit is "poured out" (Acts 2:17, 18, 33; 10:45). Fifth, the believers "receive the Holy Spirit" (Acts 2:38, 8:15, 17, 19, 10:47, 19:2). Sixth, the Holy Spirit is "given" (Acts 8:18, 11:17). Finally, the Holy Spirit "falls upon" them (Acts 8:16, 10:44, 11:15).

Hart concludes this section by saying, "Spirit Baptism in the New Testament refers to conversion-initiation, initial sanctification, and spiritual empowerment as well as the outworking of these realities in the total Christian life."[42]

You Will Receive Power

> But you will receive power when the Holy Spirit comes on you; and you will be my witnesses in Jerusalem, and in all Judea and Samaria, and to the ends of the earth. Acts 1:8

> At the present time, more and more people are anxiously asking themselves and each other whether they have the power of God in their lives, with less and less certainty in their minds as to what that might mean. J.I. Packer.[43]

There is a stirring among God's people—a hungering for more of God. The formal church processes fail to convince people that they have a real experience with God. This hungering leads many people to doubt if God exists or doubt their relationship with him. When we read the Bible, it is natural to assume that Christian life today should resemble the Christian life described and promised in the early days. It is totally lacking in satisfaction to tell people that Christianity today cannot be the same as or similar to what is described in the Bible. Such an assertion leads to the conclusion that we have transitioned from biblical Christianity to Church Christianity, where the church has replaced the Holy Spirit.

Acts 1:8 indicates that the biblical norm for all Christians is that they should have the supernatural power of the Spirit to bear witness to the Christian faith; even cessationists will agree to that.[44] The disagreements relate to when this power is received, how the power is displayed, and what it should be called. John MacArthur argues that baptism in (or with) the Spirit refers only to salvation. The "power" experience should be referred to as "filled" with the Spirit. Baptism occurs only once, but there can be many "fillings" with the Spirit.[45] As a cessationist, MacArthur further argues that the supernatural gifts ceased with the death of the last apostle, and consequently, the "power" referred to in Acts 1:8 no longer includes supernatural gifts. MacArthur's vision for the church differs significantly from the church portrayed in Acts.

In the midst of all of the doctrinal arguments about the baptism in (or with) the Spirit, one thing is undeniable. Jesus and the apostles expected the experience to result in empowerment: specifically, the power to bear witness. Although Pentecostals are right to say that the most frequent sign of this power was speaking in tongues and prophecy, we find that the apostles never directly taught that all would speak in tongues or that this was the only sign that would be acceptable. Considering that God assigns different spiritual gifts to different people for the overall benefit of the body of Christ, it seems apparent that while the purpose of the Spirit's empowerment is for bearing witness, each person's empowerment will be crafted to fit the place God has called them to serve. There is no indication that when believers "receive power," it will be manifested the same in every person. Paul's letter to the Corinthians specifically points to the differences in the manifestations of the Spirit (1 Cor. 12:4–7).

Every Christian is born of the Spirit the moment they are saved and their sins are forgiven. That is what we mean by being "born again"—to be renewed and restored by the action of the Holy Spirit. In theological terms, it is called regeneration (to be restored). The Apostle Paul declared, "If anyone does not have the Spirit of Christ, they do not belong to Christ" (Rom. 8:9). From this, we know that every Christian has "the Spirit of Christ." However, not everyone who claims to be a Christian can testify that they "received power" at the time of conversion—or at some subsequent time. To be born of the Spirit results in transformation, restoration, and renewal from the sinful, fallen nature into the nature of Christ. During the creation, God said, "Let us make man in our own image" (Gen. 1:26). Prior to the fall, Adam and Eve were created in the image of God—that does not mean their bodies or the physical image, but it means that their human

Spirit Baptism

spirit was similar in design, nature, and attitude to the Spirit of God. The human spirit has become corrupted as a result of sin, and we are all born with a selfish, sinful nature that has self-pleasure and self-preservation as its first priorities. The only way to restore and reclaim the human spirit in the image of God is by being born again through the work of the Holy Spirit.

We are "justified"—set free from the guilt of sin—when we are born again, and the restoration process begins. It begins—but does not end—the moment we are born of the Spirit. We are legally restored into the family of God, but the process of being transformed into the image of God is a lifelong journey. The Apostle Paul reminded the Romans, "Do not conform to the pattern of this world but be transformed by the renewing of your mind" (Rom. 12:2). The mind is the gateway to the human spirit, and the spirit will continue to feed upon the words, sights, and thoughts that pass through the mind. The human spirit becomes more Christlike as the mind is transformed and renewed.

In the baptism associated with the new birth, the Holy Spirit baptizes the believer into Christ. *"For we were all baptized by one Spirit so as to form one body—whether Jews or Gentiles, slave or free—and we were all given the one Spirit to drink" (1 Cor. 12:13.) "For as many of you as have been baptized into Christ have put on Christ" (Gal. 3:27)*. In the baptism that brings power, Jesus baptizes the believer by immersing them in the Holy Spirit. "John answered them all, 'I baptize you with water. But one more powerful than I will come, the thongs of whose sandals I am not worthy to untie. He will baptize you with the Holy Spirit and with fire'" (Lk. 3:16). The early apostles expected both events to happen at the same time—or at least to begin at the same time—at the new birth. Salvation is the result of being forgiven and born of the Spirit. No action taken by the church can produce salvation unless the Holy Spirit creates the new birth in the individual. That is why Paul writes, "If anyone does not have the Spirit of Christ, they do not belong to Christ" (Rom. 8:9). The new birth brings salvation and justification and begins the process of restoration.

It is clear that the twelve apostles had the Spirit at work within them during their ministry with Christ. They preached with great power, healed the sick, and cast out demons. Yet their power was a temporary delegation of spiritual authority given to them by Jesus. John wrote: "By this, he meant the Spirit, whom those who believed in him were later to receive. Up to that time, the Spirit had not been given since Jesus had not yet been glorified" (Jn. 7:39). After the resurrection, Jesus said,

> Do not leave Jerusalem, but wait for the gift my Father promised, which you have heard me speak about. For John baptized with water, but in a few days you will be baptized with the Holy Spirit . . . [and] you will receive power when the Holy Spirit comes on you. Acts 1:4–8

The New Testament, especially the Book of Acts, uses several different phrases to describe the baptism with the Spirit, including *baptized with the Spirit* (Acts 1:5, 11:16), *receive the Spirit* (Acts 2:38, 8:17, 8:19), *the Spirit comes on* (Acts 1:8, 10:44, 11:15, 19:6), and *filled with the Spirit* (Acts 2:4, 4:8, 4:31, 9:17, 13:9, 13:52).[46] What's important to note is that in each case, Spirit baptism results in an observable occurrence. The individuals knew they had experienced Spirit baptism, and in most cases, others around them observed it. It will be helpful to look at some of the biblical cases.

> The believers were filled with the Spirit and spoke in other languages. Acts 2:38

> After they prayed, the place where they were meeting was shaken. And they were all filled with the Holy Spirit and spoke the word of God boldly. Acts 4:31

Spirit Baptism

When the believers in Samaria received the Holy Spirit, others around them observed what had happened. Acts 8:17–18

When the Gentile believers at Cornelius' home received the Holy Spirit, they glorified God in different languages. Peter testified that it was similar to what the Jews had experienced at Pentecost. Acts 10:44–45 (Also see Acts 11:15 and 15:8.)

When Paul asked the believers at Ephesus if they received the Holy Spirit when they became believers, they said no. Paul then prayed for them, and they received the Holy Spirit and spoke in languages and prophesied. Some Bible scholars will argue that these men were not saved, but even after they were baptized at the hands of the apostles, they still did not receive the power of the Spirit until Paul laid his hands on them. Acts 19:1–6

My purpose in reviewing these biblical examples is not to argue that tongues is, or is not, the initial evidence, but rather to show that Spirit baptism is incomplete without the promised power.

Every believer has been baptized by the Holy Spirit into Christ, and as a result, the Holy Spirit remains with the believer to continue the restoration and transformation process. A person may be baptized by the Spirit into Christ and not experience anything dramatic, emotional, or outwardly observable. When Paul asked the people of Ephesus if they had received the Holy Spirit, they replied, "No, we have not even heard that there is a Holy Spirit" (Acts 19:2).

Many people talk about "spiritual power" while at the same time advocating for the complete cessation of miraculous gifts. Those who hold this position argue that God performed special miracles during the first century of the church (the Apostolic age) in order to build a firm foundation for the church. However, they argue that after the church was firmly established, God no longer worked in special ways to demonstrate his power through individuals. The major weakness of cessationism is that Scripture does not teach that miracles or miraculous gifts would cease to operate in the church after the death of the last apostle. If cessationism were true, it would mean that God left us with no specific instructions or blueprint on how the church should operate after the first century. The only Bible model we have of how to be and do church is the New Testament teachings of a church with a full set of spiritual gifts. We also note that such miraculous gifts were held not just by the apostles but by ordinary men and women filled with the Spirit: for example, Stephen (Acts 6:8), Philip (Acts 8:4–8), Philip's four daughters (Acts 21:9), and the prophets in the church at Jerusalem (Acts 11:27). If God intended for such gifts to be removed, it would seem that He would have given us instructions on how the church should conduct itself after the removal of such gifts rather than leaving us to our own man-made ways of doing church. We find ourselves, then, in a position in which we talk about being filled with the power of the Holy Spirit, but we don't want or expect the Holy Spirit to do anything significant and observable.

It is interesting to compare the views of John MacArthur and John Piper because they are close friends and colleagues. MacArthur is a very outspoken critic of those who believe in supernatural gifts, yet he rightly confirms that being filled with the Spirit is an experience subsequent to salvation that results in spiritual power. However, the power he describes relates to the building of a godly character but excludes supernatural gifts. Piper disagrees with MacArthur regarding spiritual gifts. Piper describes himself as a "continuationist"—one who believes that the supernatural gifts of the Spirit remain in operation today.[47] He indicates his evolving theology in a blog post in which he states that he is increasingly drawn to the belief that baptism by the Spirit into the body of Christ (new birth) and the Spirit baptism in Acts 2 are different, the latter being a special empowerment for Christian ministry. Piper writes, "So here is my conclusion: being baptized with the Holy Spirit is when a believer in Jesus Christ receives extraordinary power for Christ-exalting ministry." Regardless of what term we use—*baptized in the Spirit* or *filled with the Spirit*—the term is less important than the result. Larry Hart, like most Charismatics, prefers to stay with the term *baptized in the Spirit*, but he is clear that the meaning includes initiation into Christ (salvation) and empowerment for Christian service, and it refers to the entirety of the Christian life.[48] The main thing that differentiates a Charismatic believer from a non-Charismatic believer is that the Charismatic seeks after God with a supernatural worldview that invites the believer to participate in what God is doing in the church and the world.

My conclusion on this complex issue is that the many examples in Acts clearly demonstrate that the Holy Spirit blows where and when he wishes (Jn. 3:8), and God the Holy Spirit is not limited to one method of operation. The Reformers (Luther and Calvin) attempted to define the *ordo salutis*—the order in which salvation-related events take place. The Book of Acts makes it clear that there is no fixed *ordo salutis* in the Spirit's work. But we can be sure that when the Spirit comes in his fullness, he brings power into the life of the believer. That power may be displayed differently in different people because each one has a unique calling to fulfill. The power is not for our own benefit but for the benefit of Christ and his church.

The Holy Spirit and the Human Spirit

> Jesus answered, "Very truly I tell you, no one can enter the kingdom of God unless they are born of water and the Spirit. Flesh gives birth to flesh, but *the Spirit gives birth to spirit*. You should not be surprised at my saying, 'You must be born again.' The wind blows wherever it pleases. You hear its sound, but you cannot tell where it comes from or where it is going. So it is with everyone born of the Spirit." Jn. 3:5–8

The Spirit gives birth to spirit—the Holy Spirit produces a reborn human spirit. Nicodemus wanted to understand Jesus' words about being born again. Nicodemus thought Jesus was referring to physical birth, but Jesus was talking about a rebirth of the human spirit. During the new birth process, a marriage-like union takes place between the Holy Spirit and the human spirit. We are united with Christ through his Spirit and placed into the body of Christ, which is the mystical body of Christ, the mystical church.

The Greek word *pneuma* can mean spirit, breath, or wind;[49] only the context can tell us what the author had in mind. Even in cases where the apparent meaning is spirit, it could mean the human spirit, Holy Spirit, or simply an attitude. In some cases, *pneuma* may be preceded by the adjective *hagios* (holy), and we know that it is a reference to the Holy Spirit, but sometimes *pneuma* clearly means Holy Spirit even without the adjective. The Greek New Testament did not use capital letters to distinguish between the Holy Spirit and the human spirit; this distinction was added by some English translations to indicate whether the reference is to the Holy Spirit (capital S) or the human spirit (small s). Only the context in which it is used may reveal what the writer had in mind, and the various translations do not always agree. Gordon Fee sometimes uses the term *Spirit/spirit* to denote that the Greek text could be either/or. Fee states that God may have used these terms in this way to show that the union between the human spirit and the Holy Spirit is so complete that the two spirits—human and Holy—are indistinguishable.[50] For example, in 1 Corinthians 14, in which the subject is praying in tongues, Paul writes,

> For if I pray in a tongue, my spirit prays, but my mind is unfruitful. So what shall I do? I will pray with my spirit, but I will also pray with my understanding; I will sing with my spirit, but I will also sing with my understanding. 1 Cor. 14:14–15

Paul is stating that when he prays in tongues, his human spirit is praying under the direction of the Holy Spirit, but his mind is unfruitful—his mind doesn't understand what he is saying, but the Spirit does. Fee writes, "Thus he means 'my S/spirit prays/sings' in the sense that his own spirit is worshipping, but this transpires by the direct influence of the indwelling Spirit of God."[51] George Ladd agrees:

Spirit Baptism

"In the discussion of glossolalia, man's spirit is even differentiated from his mind (1 Cor. 14:14)."[52] The union between the Holy Spirit and the human spirit is like the marriage between a husband and wife; they become one.

Theologically, we know that the supernatural power flows from the divine Spirit; it is not of human origin. Yet the human person may not be aware of any division between their thoughts and the divine illumination of the Spirit. Paul writes, concerning his own work, "For God is my witness, whom I serve with my spirit in the gospel of his Son" (Rom 8:1). Certainly, Paul is not serving God in his human spirit acting alone, but in union with the Holy Spirit, the two spirits become indistinguishable in their work.

In the Gospel of John, we find Jesus having a conversation with the woman from Samaria:

> [19] "Sir," the woman said, "I can see that you are a prophet. [20]. Our ancestors worshiped on this mountain, but you Jews claim that the place where we must worship is in Jerusalem."
>
> [21] "Woman," Jesus replied, "believe me, a time is coming when you will worship the Father neither on this mountain nor in Jerusalem. [22] You Samaritans worship what you do not know; we worship what we do know, for salvation is from the Jews. [23] Yet a time is coming and has now come when the true worshipers will worship the Father in the Spirit and in truth, for they are the kind of worshipers the Father seeks. [24] God is spirit, and his worshipers must worship in the Spirit and in truth." Jn. 4:19–24

In verses 23 and 24, Jesus says, "The true worshipers will worship the Father *in the Spirit* and in truth, for they are the kind of worshipers the Father seeks. *God is spirit*, and his worshipers must worship *in the Spirit* and in truth." The Greek text does not use any adjectives in these two verses—it does not say Holy Spirit or human spirit. The NIV assumes the first and third are references to the Holy Spirit, and the middle reference is to a general type of spirit—but no specific spirit. The ASV takes the opposite approach, assuming that the first and third are references to the human spirit, and the middle reference is to the Holy Spirit. Craig Keener refers to this passage as "worship empowered by the Spirit."[53] He acknowledges the possibility of the first and third occurrences of *pneuma* being a reference to the human spirit, but he argues that this would not be John's normal usage of the word *Spirit*.[54] Leon Morris' approach seems to be more consistent with the Johannine use of *pneuma*: "One must worship, not simply outwardly by being in the right place and taking the right attitude, but in one's spirit."[55] To worship in one's spirit (the human spirit) is not a reference to place nor to the human spirit in isolation; rather, it is an integration of Spirit and spirit. Ladd finds that "because man is *pneuma*, he is capable of receiving the divine *pneuma* and thus coming into a close relationship with God."[56] Westcott describes spirit (*pneuma*) as that part of man's nature which holds or is capable of holding, intercourse with the eternal order. The spirit in man responds to the Spirit of God. . . . The sphere of worship was, therefore, now to be that highest region where the divine and human meet."[57]

The human spirit died in its relationship with God when Adam and Eve sinned. God warned Adam, "You are free to eat from any tree in the garden; but you must not eat from the tree of the knowledge of good and evil, for when you eat from it, you will certainly die" (Gen. 1:16–17). This death was not a physical death but a spiritual death—the death of the human spirit in its relationship with God. This is why God said to Nicodemus, "You must be born again" (Jn. 3:7). The spirit that died in the garden is born again through Christ. In the natural person—one without Christ—there is often conflict between the spirit and the soul. The soul is the center of our feelings and emotions, while the spirit is that part of the human designed to be in the image of God and to communicate with God. In the person who has not been born again, or even in the carnal Christian, the feelings and the emotions located in the soul will influence the person's thoughts and actions. After the new birth, the human spirit will be in union with the Holy Spirit and will attempt to transform the thoughts and emotions of the soul. The mind becomes the battleground as the emotions and desires press in on it. The person must make conscious decisions to seek after God and give the work of the Spirit/spirit priority.[58] A host of forces—internal and external—influence the soul and create a battleground for control of one's life. Paul recounts this battle when he writes:

> I do not understand what I do. For what I want to do I do not do, but what I hate, I do. And if I do what I do not want to do, I agree that the law is good. As it is, it is no longer I myself who do it, but it is sin living in me. For I know that good itself does not dwell in me, that is, in my sinful nature. For I have the desire to do what is good, but I cannot carry it out. For I do not do the good I want to do, but the evil I do not want to do—this I keep on doing. Rom. 7:15–19

> The mind governed by the flesh [carnal mind] is death, but the mind governed by the Spirit is life and peace. Rom. 8:6

The mind is the product of the influences that shape it. A carnal mind (a mind governed by the flesh) is a mind in which the soul, with its feelings and emotions, has priority. The spiritual mind is that mind that is continuously being shaped by the Spirit. The union between God and mankind occurs in the human spirit, and from there, it is able to penetrate the soul. The soul is not evil, but it must be trained to become godly. The voice of the Holy Spirit speaks through the human spirit, and the free will of the human mind must give priority to what the Spirit/spirit is saying.

The Release of the Spirit

Watchman Nee reminds us that because the Holy Spirit and the human spirit are joined together in a union like a marriage, their work is sometimes indistinguishable when it is worked through a human vessel.[59] When we think about spiritual gifts, especially the oral gifts such as prophecy, the human spirit and the Holy Spirit work together such that what the person speaks forth are actually the words and work of the Spirit. Nee says that we must become broken and our flesh (soul) must be put to death (Gal. 5:24) so that the spirit (the human spirit joined to the Holy Spirit) can live. When the old nature is put to death, then the new nature can live. It is then that the Holy Spirit and the human spirit can go forth together and minister to the body of Christ. When the woman with the issue of blood touched Jesus' garment, she was healed (Lk. 8); Jesus asked the crowd around him, "Who touched me?" When no one responded, Jesus said, "Someone touched me; I know that power has gone out from me" (Lk. 8:46). Jesus experienced power going out from his body when the woman touched him in faith. This was an automatic action triggered by her faith. When the human spirit has been born anew by the Holy Spirit, the two go out together according to God's sovereign will to do his work. But the human spirit joined with the Holy Spirit is not released to go out on mission unless the outer person (the carnal-soulish nature) has become broken, and the new person is in control.

Tares Among the Wheat

When Paul says, "And if anyone does not have the Spirit of Christ, they do not belong to Christ" (Rom. 8:9b), he makes two assertions. First, he asserts that everyone who belongs to Christ does have the Spirit. Second—and just as important—he asserts that a person without the Spirit is not a Christian. The person without the Spirit may go through all the motions of being a Christian—confession, baptism, church membership—and not really be a Christian because they do not have the Spirit. The Parable of the Tares teaches us that there are people "in the kingdom" who look like true believers, but they are not;

they are imposters (Matt. 13:24-43). Jesus said, "The tares [weeds] are the people of the evil one"—they appear to be in the kingdom, but they are not true sons of the King (Matt. 13:37-42). Romans 8 does not declare that everyone in the church has the Spirit; it says that those without the Spirit do not truly belong to Christ. Some imposters are aware that they are not genuine, but some are self-deceived. They believe they are Christians because they checked all the boxes, but their repentance and confession are not genuine; they simply followed someone else's example or instruction. We should be careful not to place someone in a leadership position who has no genuine display of the Spirit's work in their life.

Summary

To be born of the Spirit (Jn. 3:8) renders the believer alive in Christ through the Holy Spirit. The believer is incorporated into the church—the Body of Christ—and the Holy Spirit dwells within. Being born of the Spirit may result in the Spirit's power only when the individual fully surrenders to the Spirit. The power is not static—it flows like a stream (sometimes a mighty rushing stream)—according to the needs of the time and the sovereignty of God. In the new birth, the human spirit is brought to life such that the human spirit and the Holy Spirit become united inside the believer. The union between the Holy Spirit and the human spirit is so complete that they can work as one. Spiritual gifts are accomplished by the Holy Spirit and the human spirit working together.

The view held by most Charismatics is that we receive the Holy Spirit at the time of salvation. However, a person may receive (and should seek after) additional spiritual experiences, which may be described as baptisms or fillings with the Spirit. The term *baptism in* (or *with*) *the Spirit* is a metaphor that implies a complete immersion in the Spirit to the point of overflowing. These additional experiences are for the purpose of spiritual transformation and empowerment for service. The key verse that describes this experience is Acts 1:8. "You will receive power when the Holy Spirit comes on you; and you will be my witnesses in Jerusalem, and in all Judea and Samaria, and to the ends of the earth."

Some may receive a spiritual baptism like a mighty rushing wind with tongues of fire (Acts 2:2), and others may receive a baptism that is less dramatic, but the results will be similar—you will receive power to serve God supernaturally. The power of the Spirit may be manifested differently through various individuals according to their gifts. Some gifts may appear like natural talents (for example, gifts of teaching, giving, or hospitality), and other gifts may appear more spectacular and miraculous. Regardless of whether the gift appears spectacular or ordinary, the power and the results are from God.

Chapter 3
Spiritual Gifts

> Now about the gifts of the Spirit, brothers and sisters,
> I do not want you to be uninformed. 1 Cor. 12:1

Spiritual gifts are of great importance to Charismatics; for many, the very word *Charismatic* is summed up by "emphasis on supernatural gifts." Such gifts represent the dividing line between Charismatics and cessationists.[60] To say that spiritual gifts are "all-important" to Charismatics would be an overstatement. As shown in Chapter 1 of this book, there are many attributes of what it means to be Charismatic, not just gifts of the Spirit. Also among the misconceptions is the idea that speaking in tongues is the all-important gift. Assemblies of God theologian Donald Gee lamented that in the Pentecostal outpouring that began just after 1900, there was an overemphasis on the gift of tongues and an underemphasis on the other gifts.[61] Gee points out that the original purpose of the spiritual gifts seems to have been to confirm the preaching of the Word; thus, Gee elevates preaching and teaching to a higher place of priority as gifts that buildup the body of Christ.

What Are Spiritual Gifts?

Spiritual gifts are the work of the Spirit through a believer. They are not human talents, abilities, or skills. Spiritual gifts are not distinct objects that are dropped into a person's life; they are simply ways of describing how God works through the believer. A gift is a "manifestation" of the Spirit's power (1 Cor. 12:8). Since all believers have the Holy Spirit (Rom. 8:9), manifestations of the Spirit's power can be displayed in every Christian's life. Sam Storms says concerning spiritual gifts, "This supernatural and divine energy or power quite literally fills and indwells the body and soul of every born-again believer."[62] God chooses how and when he wants to display his power according to his sovereign will (1 Cor. 12:11).

There are several lists of spiritual gifts in the Bible; the lists are examples and not comprehensive.[63] One cannot list or describe all the ways God might choose to manifest his power—we can only give examples.

Romans 12:6–8	1 Corinthians 12:8:10	Ephesians 4:11
Prophesying	Word of wisdom	Apostles
Serving	Word of knowledge	Prophets
Teaching	Faith	Evangelists
Encouraging	Gifts of healing	Pastors
Giving	Miracles	Teachers
Leading	Prophecy	
(Administration)	Discerning of spirits	
Showing mercy	Speaking in tongues (languages)	
	Interpretation of tongues (languages)	

The ministries listed in Ephesians are ministry callings and not singular gifts. For example, a pastor will have several gifts, including teaching and leadership. An apostle or prophet undoubtedly will have multiple gifts. Although a ministry calling is broader than a single gift, they are usually listed in the gifts because they operate in the same way.

Spiritual Gifts

God does not simply drop a spiritual gift into your life. A gift is simply a manifestation of the Spirit who dwells in you. It is identified as a spiritual gift when the same type of manifestation occurs on a somewhat regular basis. One person may prophesy on rare occasions, but the true prophet will prophesy more frequently and with greater specificity. One person may pray for someone to be healed and see dramatic results on rare occasions, but the gifted person will see such results more frequently as a result of their gift. Every person may share their faith and may see others come to Christ from time to time, but the evangelist will have much greater success in winning people to Christ. Everyone is called to give financially, but the person with the gift of giving will have more resources (from God) and will have a willing heart to give (Rom. 12:8). Every spiritual gift is supernaturally empowered and resourced by God.

Gift Groups

We have already noted that the lists of gifts presented in Scripture are examples and not exhaustive; we might also note that a gift or set of gifts might work differently through one person than through another.

> There are different kinds of gifts, but the same
> Spirit distributes them. There are different kinds of
> service, but the same Lord. There are different kinds
> of working, but in all of them and in everyone, it is
> the same God at work. 1 Cor. 12:4–6

There are several different groups of gifts that are similar in nature and may be indistinguishable at times.

Prophetic Gifts

Word of knowledge, word of wisdom, discerning of spirits, and prophecy are all types of revelation gifts. If we follow the classical definitions,[64] a word of knowledge is speaking something that the person could not have known on their own. In a very similar manner, a word of wisdom involves speaking something that includes wisdom on a specific topic—such as the mysteries of God—and includes information the person would not have known without divine revelation. It is *word of wisdom* and *word of knowledge* because the Greek text includes the words *logos* (word or message), *logos sophia*, and *logos gnosis*. Discerning of spirits also involves the Spirit of God revealing something to a gifted person, but it is different in that it doesn't necessarily require that the gift result in a "logos" being given forth. In reality, all of these are limited forms of the gift of prophecy. The Old Testament prophets spoke with specific knowledge and wisdom as a result of their prophetic gifts, and they did not distinguish between them. It may seem strange to include "encouraging" in the prophetic gifts, but Paul writes, "But the one who prophesies speaks to people for their strengthening, encouraging, and comfort" (1 Cor. 14:3). One form of prophecy is to speak words under the inspiration of the Spirit to strengthen, encourage, and comfort others. Nearly all Christians will do this from time to time, but the person with the gift does it more frequently and with greater results than a person without the gift.

We also see revelatory gifts at work through Daniel as he and his colleagues had gifts of knowledge and the interpretation of dreams. "To these four young men God gave knowledge and understanding of all kinds of literature and learning; and Daniel could understand visions and dreams of all kinds" (Dan. 1:17). Tongues and interpretation are also in the revelation group when they are used together. Paul indicates that tongues and interpretation are the equivalent of prophecy when the message in tongues is interpreted (1 Cor. 14:6). Joel's prophecy, which Peter repeated on the Day of Pentecost (Joel 2:28; Acts 2:17), indicates that dreams and visions are to be a normal part of the New Testament church.

Power Gifts

The Corinthian list includes miracles, healing, and faith. Jesus taught us that through faith, a person can do all things, including healing the sick (Matt. 17:19–20). So, a person with great faith could heal the sick, and a person with the gift of miracles could also heal the sick. The gifts of healing are a specific type of faith or miracle gift (the word *gifts* is plural). Faith can result in instantaneous action, such as healing, or it can result in believing God over a period of time. George Mueller established several homes for orphans in England (1835–1870). There were many days when there was not enough money or food to feed the orphans, and George Muller and his wife would pray and leave it in God's hands. On many occasions, the food or money would arrive just at mealtime. This happened very frequently, and the staff was often distressed, but Muller relied totally upon prayer even when mealtime arrived, and there was nothing to feed the children— but it always arrived at the right time. By faith, Elijah caused an axe head to float (2 Kgs. 6:1–6), and he also raised the dead (1 Kgs. 17:21–22). Elijah's faith and George Muller's faith were both supernatural, but the two men used their gifts in different ways based on the needs of the time. As a prophet, Elijah's gifts included faith, miracles, healing, and prophecy. The same gift mix can be seen in the life of the apostles, especially Paul and Peter. Peter exercised the gift of wisdom (Acts 2:14–41), healed the sick (Acts 3:1–10, 5:15), and raised the dead (Acts 9:40–43). As with the revelation gifts, the power gifts are so similar that they could be used interchangeably in many cases. All miracles are manifestations of the Spirit of God and therefore are subject to the sovereign will of God. Every spiritual gift, especially the power gifts, must be accompanied by wisdom and discernment to know the will of God concerning the use of the gift.

Teaching and Preaching

Although these gifts are not mentioned in the Corinthian list, they are functions within the church, as found in Ephesians 4. Some would argue that ministries and gifts are different, but I find no reason to make that distinction. No one can dispute that God empowers preaching and teaching. Preaching could be considered a form of prophecy, and teaching relies upon wisdom, but both preaching and teaching are Spirit-empowered and meet the general definition of spiritual gifts. An ability is only a spiritual gift when it is a manifestation of the Spirit. An eloquent speaker may draw crowds and stir people's emotions, but that does not make it a spiritual gift. If God is the power behind the gift, we would also expect to see supernatural results. However, missionaries have sometimes labored for many years of faithful preaching with no visible results until a breakthrough was achieved. The fruit of our labors, even when empowered by the Holy Spirit, may sometimes be delayed.

Serving Gifts

The serving gifts are found mostly in Romans 12, and they include serving, giving, leading (or administration), and showing mercy. Hospitality is also frequently recognized as a gift, although it is not specifically called a gift.[65] A great example of serving gifts is found in the Old Testament. God instructed Moses to build a mobile tabernacle for use while they traveled through the wilderness, but no one had the skills to build it according to God's instructions.

> Then Moses said to the Israelites, "See, the Lord has chosen Bezalel son of Uri, the son of Hur, of the tribe of Judah, and he has filled him with the Spirit of God, with wisdom, with understanding, with knowledge and with all kinds of skills—to make artistic designs for work in gold, silver and bronze, to cut and set stones, to work in wood and to engage in all kinds of artistic crafts. And he has given both him and Oholiab, son of Ahisamak, of the tribe of Dan, the ability to teach others. He has filled them with the skill to do all kinds of work as engravers, designers, embroiderers in blue, purple, and scarlet yarn and fine linen, and weavers—all of them skilled workers and designers." Ex. 35:30–35

Spiritual Gifts

The gifts given to these men may not seem supernatural or spectacular, but the knowledge and skill were given by God—and that fits the definition of a spiritual gift. It also shows that gifts require human effort under the control and empowerment of the Spirit.

As can be seen, some spiritual gifts have normal human counterparts; that is, the gift may appear the same as a human ability except that a gift is empowered and resourced by God. Examples include serving, teaching, encouraging, giving, leading, and showing mercy. Some great leaders have been tyrants, and their leadership ability was certainly not a spiritual gift. Likewise, a philanthropist may give large amounts of money and not be a Christian. A great singer or musician may not be a Christian, but a Christian who acknowledges that God has given them a gift has a responsibility to treat it as a spiritual gift and not as a commercial product to be marketed.

Desiring and Acquiring Spiritual Gifts

There is a common misperception that all the spiritual gifts you will ever receive are given at the moment of salvation (or at the moment of Spirit baptism), and one's spiritual gifts never change over time. There are several factors that determine what gifts we have: (1) the sovereign choice of God, (2) the needs of the local body as evaluated by God, (3) our desires to serve, and (4) our level of grace (spiritual maturity).

God's sovereign choice is the most important factor because he makes the ultimate decision in what gifts a person will have (1 Cor. 12:11). However, God chooses in accordance with the needs of the church (1 Cor. 12:7). These are macro-level decisions on God's part. He does not send a new gifted person to a local congregation just because that congregation wants to start a new program, and they want a capable person to lead it. Some very good churches and ministry programs fail (at least from a human perspective) while others continue to grow. When Jesus said, "I will build my church, and the gates of hades will not overcome it" (Matt. 16:18), he did not guarantee the success of every local church. Jesus is more concerned with the overall health of the kingdom of God. He may allow one congregation to suffer persecution and closure of the church because the kingdom is locked in a spiritual battle with the forces of darkness. In every battle, there are some casualties, even though God controls the final outcome. Jesus expressed sorrow when John the Baptist was executed, but the kingdom continued to grow and win victories. Peter and Paul were both martyred, and they did not use their spiritual gifts to save themselves from persecution. God grants gifts for the "common good," but he doesn't fill every need identified in the local church. God works in a more strategic direction according to his plan for the kingdom. There seem to have been more prophets in the church at Jerusalem and Antioch (Acts 11:27, 13:1) than most other churches, but that was God's sovereign choice. Antioch was second only to Corinth in their use and understanding of spiritual gifts. The needs of the body may change from time to time, and God can certainly develop additional gifts as the needs of the church change. Local churches in Paul's time were mostly house churches with about twelve to thirty people. Many churches today are in the tens of thousands in average weekly attendance. God grants gifts to individuals according to his sovereign will and the needs of the church, and those needs may change from time to time. The example of the craftsmen whom God filled with his Spirit and empowered to build the tabernacle is a great example of gifts added in a time of need (Exodus 35:30–35).

In addition to the needs of the body (the universal body, not just the local body), God's sovereign choice also allows for individual factors. In this broad category, we will consider Paul's admonition that we pray for and earnestly desire spiritual gifts, that gifts are allocated according to the level of grace in the individual, and that gifts can go unused, and we need to stir up the gift.

> Follow the way of love and eagerly desire gifts of the
> Spirit, especially prophecy. 1 Cor. 14:1

Spiritual Gifts

> Since you are eager for gifts of the Spirit, try to excel in those that build up the church. 1 Cor. 14:12

> For this reason, the one who speaks in a tongue should pray that they may interpret what they say. 1 Cor. 14:13

> Therefore, my brothers and sisters, be eager to prophesy. 1 Cor. 14:39

The Apostle encourages us to *eagerly desire, pray for, and try to excel* concerning spiritual gifts. Paul would not have given these instructions if our desires and prayers had no effect on God's choice in granting a gift. Our desires are subject to God's final sovereignty, but he invites us to pray and desire. Throughout 1 Corinthians 14, Paul admonishes us to seek those gifts that are most profitable in building up the church: "Since you are eager for gifts of the Spirit, try to excel in *those that build up the church*" (1 Cor. 14:12). The use of spiritual gifts within the body is for the "common good" of the body (1 Cor. 12:7). Any desire to have a gift for our own personal benefit or pride will certainly not be honored by God.

"Do not neglect your gift, which was given you through prophecy when the body of elders laid their hands on you" (1 Tim. 4:14). "For this reason, I remind you to fan into flame the gift of God, which is in you through the laying on of my hands" (2 Tim. 1:6). Paul's advice to Timothy is a reminder that spiritual gifts can be neglected and need to be stirred up or fanned into flame (reactivated). Scripture tells us we are stewards of God's grace (1 Pet. 4:10; Eph. 3:2). Stewardship means that something belonging to God has been entrusted to us, and we are responsible for the administration of that gift for the benefit of others. This human responsibility begins with our concern for the members of the church; we seek those gifts that will best benefit others, and we use our gifts for their benefit. There is a common misperception that all spiritual gifts are totally controlled by the Holy Spirit, and the human person has no control of or responsibility for their actions or words. Paul reminds us that "the spirits of the prophets are under the control of the prophets" (1 Cor. 14:32). He is telling the Corinthians that even while prophesying, the person remains in control of their actions, and all things must be done for the benefit of the church. Specifically, in this context, Paul is telling those with the gift of prophecy not to speak out of order, and they must respect the time and ministries of others in the church. The Holy Spirit does not compel or force a person to deliver their prophetic message at a particular time. Some messages are better saved until the right time and place to deliver them. There may be occasions when the Spirit takes control of a person's body, but that is not the norm.

Our conclusion in this section on desiring and acquiring spiritual gifts is that we have the Holy Spirit from the time of conversion, but the manifestations of the Spirit, vis-a-vis spiritual gifts, are subject to the ongoing decisions and callings of God upon the believer. Gifts may be added or taken away from time to time. Gifts may also be developed. Elijah and Elisha were headmasters of groups of prophets, sometimes known as "the school of the prophets" (1 Sam. 19:20; 2 Kgs. 2:3, 4:38). No one can teach the gift of prophecy, but the senior prophets taught the younger ones how to properly administer their gifts. Paul's instructions found in 1 Corinthians chapters 12 and 14 are primarily concerned with how spiritual gifts are used within the church. This implies that the gifts—including those that are sometimes considered ecstatic—such as tongues, interpretation, and prophecy—are still under the control of the person, and people with such gifts must learn and grow in maturity in how they use their gifts.

> We have different gifts, according to the grace given to each of us. If your gift is prophesying, then prophesy in accordance with your faith. Rom. 12:6

In God's sovereign decision over what gifts to grant, the spiritual maturity of the person is taken into consideration. Gifts are given according to the measure of grace (or maturity) and readiness to handle the gift. God has no desire to grant a spiritual gift to a person who is not spiritually mature enough to handle it, and yet we know that some do receive gifts and yet fall into ruin. Not everyone with a gift will manifest that gift in the same way. Paul tells us that a person with the gift of prophecy should prophesy in accordance with their level of faith. A person may have the gift in its embryo form, but the gift may not be developed to full maturity. That person is not an Elijah or a Jeremiah; they should speak only that which the Spirit has absolutely made clear to them.

Discovering the Spirit and His Gifts

There are many books on how to discover your spiritual gift, but I suggest that our awareness of our spiritual gifts flows from our awareness of the Spirit himself. The more intimate we are with the Spirit, the more aware we will be of his desire to work through us with his gifts. The Samaritan believers (Acts 8:14–17) and the Ephesian believers (Acts 19:6) were baptized believers, but they lacked any experience with the Holy Spirit. Many people today cannot testify that the Spirit is actively working in their life. This does not mean that everyone should have daily experiences of dramatic outbursts; it means that the Spirit makes transformative changes in the way we think, desire, and believe. We should, at the very least, experience the Spirit in some knowable way.

Since the primary purpose of the gifts is to serve others, the Spirit will develop within each believer a desire to serve. In most cases, the desire will align with God's sovereign choice concerning how he wants to use us in the church. The best way to discover your spiritual gift is by developing your awareness of the Holy Spirit's presence in your life. Your relationship with God is built on a foundation of his love and grace, and our response is developed through prayer and knowledge of him. When Jesus appointed his twelve apostles, he did so "that they might be with him and that he might send them out to preach" (Mk. 3:14). Their first calling was to "be with him." Spending time with him was a prerequisite to going out on preaching missions. Spiritual gifts are not our possessions; they are demonstrations of God at work through us. God works through his chosen ones—those with whom he has an intimate relationship—not through strangers. This intimacy is developed through prayer, meditating on his Word, and in fellowship with other mature believers. No one is qualified to exercise spiritual gifts unless they have first developed an intimate relationship with Christ and his Spirit. More about this will be found in the chapter on spirituality.

There are many "gift tests" to help you discover your gift. Most of them are designed to help you identify the things you have tried and have been successful at doing or that people told you that you are good at. The problem is that they don't differentiate between a spiritual gift and a natural talent. Anything you are good at and enjoy doing will score high on a gift test. The other problem is that it doesn't identify anything you have never done before. If God calls you to be a prophet and you take a gift test prior to ever prophesying, it will not show up. There is nothing "spiritual" about those kinds of tests. That is not to say they are totally worthless. A true spiritual gift will have favorable results and will eventually be acknowledged by other Christians. I would just caution you against relying too much on gift tests or surveys.

I want to suggest three ways of identifying your spiritual gifts after you have developed an awareness and intimacy with the Spirit himself. First, be aware of how the Spirit is leading you—what is he calling you to do regarding serving others? As you grow in your spiritual awareness, you will become more certain of how God is leading you. Since none of us are infallible, you will make mistakes, and you will not always be successful. John Wimber, the founder of the Vineyard Association of Churches, encouraged people to experiment with different spiritual gifts to find out what works. A word of caution must be given here; if you want to experiment concerning giving or encouraging others or leadership, that is fine. But gifts like prophecy and interpretation are very different. A person who purports to prophesy just to experiment to see if they have that gift is doing a very dangerous experiment that may cause harm to themselves and others. Paul cautions us, "If your gift is prophesying, then prophesy in accordance with your faith" (Rom. 12:6). In most cases, a gift should be exercised under the guidance of the spiritual leadership of a local church. Paul states, "Two or three prophets should speak, and the others should weigh carefully what is said" (1 Cor. 14:29). The NASB reads "Let the others pass judgment." Even among those who are legitimate prophets, the other elders are to evaluate what is being said. Spiritual gifts do not imply that the believer is infallible while exercising the gift. However, that does not give the person a license to speak beyond their level of grace and faith. The elders should warn and, if necessary, censor those who cause confusion in the body. The Spirit is perfect, but our understanding of him is not perfect. However, God does speak and lead, and his leading is our primary way of knowing his will for our lives in areas in which individual guidance is required. God's leading is to have priority, and success and confirmation from others should follow.

Second, as in all matters, you should seek the advice of others in the church, especially those in positions of spiritual leadership. A Charismatic church must give high priority to encouraging and advising members of the body in listening to the voice of the Spirit and in the use of their spiritual gifts. Paul wrote to Timothy, saying, "Do not neglect your gift, which was given to you through prophecy when the body of elders laid their hands on you" (1 Tim. 4:14). There is no reason to limit the application of this verse to the original context because an "apostle" was present; Paul's emphasis is on the "body of elders." Prophecy in the form of wisdom and spiritual discernment should be at work in every Charismatic church. One cannot legitimately exercise a spiritual gift in a local church without the blessing and confirmation of the elders. Elders are placed in their position by God and given the authority and responsibility for sound doctrine and orderliness in the church. If the elders are in the Spirit as they should be, they will assist each member in identifying and developing their gifts. There may be times when God is leading you in a direction that no one else can see or understand, but this requires a level of maturity to ensure that God is leading and not just your own stubbornness in not wanting to submit to others in the body.

Third, true gifts will be powered by the Spirit and will produce fruit. This does not mean that everything you do will be successful. You may preach sermons that go unappreciated. You may serve others, and they respond with spite. You may seek to encourage others, and they continue in negative despondency. You may prophesy, and the people will not heed the prophecy. However, if you are faithful and obedient, there will eventually be positive fruit. Sometimes your friends and advisers—including elders—may be wrong and give you wrong advice, but your calling and your faithfulness belong to God, and he will reward you with fruit.

Dreams, Visions, and Revelations

> In the last days, God says, I will pour out my Spirit on all people. Your sons and daughters will prophesy, your young men will see visions, your old men will dream dreams. Even on my servants, both men and women, I will pour out my Spirit in those days, and they will prophesy. Acts 2:17–18

Joel's prophecy indicates that dreams, visions, and prophetic revelations should be commonplace in the New Testament church, and yet these seem to be neglected areas of the Christian experience. As with all spiritual gifts and experiences, if something is neglected, it will soon atrophy and need to be "stirred up" to be reactivated. Paul told Timothy, "Fan into flame [stir up] the gift of God, which is in you" (2 Tim. 1:6). The ability to receive and interpret dreams and visions may have been lost to the church because we have neglected something God gave to the early church. More research—through prayer and fasting—needs to be done concerning dreams and visions. The little bit that has been written on the subject tends to default to secular psychology, citing Freud and others. Freud developed the

Spiritual Gifts

theory that dreams come from two sources: the primary source being experiences from our childhood, especially suppressed thoughts and desires. Second are more recent experiences we were not able to bring to completion, and we have an inner desire to continue the experience. While this may be true of psychological dreams, it does not explain spiritual dreams. Freud attempted to compile a catalog of dream symbols with the idea that the meaning of the symbols would be universally applicable. However, even for human dreams, contemporary scientists are unable to substantiate Freud's theories, and consequently, very little reliable research is available.[66] The larger problem with all secular theories is that God is not the source of such dreams, and they have no spiritual meaning.

While we admit that more research needs to be done, some observations can be offered. Spiritual dreams come from God. Continuing the theme expressed above—that the Holy Spirit and the human spirit work together to produce gifts—it seems apparent that dreams and visions work in the same way. The Holy Spirit produces the spiritual dream within the human spirit, and from there, it finds its way to the mind as a "dream thought," much the same way psychological dreams are displayed, but the source is different. The interpretation of dreams and visions occurs in the same way; the interpretation is from the Holy Spirit passed through the human spirit. Paul says that when he prays in tongues, his spirit prays, but his mind does not understand unless the prayer is interpreted (1 Cor. 14:14). Paul is clear that some spiritual matters originate in the human spirit rather than the human mind. We can also conclude that if spiritual gifts can be developed and fanned into flame, the ability to receive and interpret dreams and visions follows the same pattern. This means the human spirit can be trained to communicate with the Holy Spirit. We recognize that the Holy Spirit is sovereign; we cannot force or manipulate Him to create a dream or vision. Nor should we expect spiritual dreams to occur every day or night. The examples we find in Scripture were usually for a significant event in the work of God that he wanted to reveal to his chosen instruments. However, Joel's prophecy indicates that revelations of this type were to be more common in the New Testament than they were in the Old Testament.

Summary

Spiritual gifts are God's normal method of doing his work in the church; he works by empowering and leading people to be his instruments. As Peter states, we are "stewards" of God's grace (1 Pet. 4:10). Gifts are not tangible objects; they are manifestations of God's work as they occur through human instruments. As manifestations of God's power, gifts are subject to God's control, but since he grants stewardship to us, he also grants that we have the ability to administer the gifts given to us (1 Cor. 14:32–33).

God is always at work in his church and in the world, and he calls us to come alongside him and join him in his work. Just as any work requires different tools for different tasks, God's work requires different gifts or manifestations of the Spirit to meet the various needs that may come about in the church. The Bible provides examples of some of the spiritual gifts that were prevalent in the first-century church, but that does not mean that spiritual gifts are limited to those examples. We are encouraged to pray for and seek after the spiritual gifts that will be most beneficial to the church (1 Cor. 12:31, 14:1, 14:39).

Dozens of books and "gift tests" have been written to help people discover their spiritual gifts. However, in this chapter, I have suggested that the best way to discover your spiritual gifts is by focusing on your awareness of the Holy Spirit's presence in your life and following the advice and wise discernment of others in your local church, especially the elders. One of the chief responsibilities of elders in a Charismatic church is to help people discover and grow in their spiritual gifts. The elders should wisely shepherd and encourage people in all areas of their spiritual growth and development, taking corrective action as necessary with the goal of growing in grace for the individual and the upbuilding of the church.

Chapter 4
Supernatural Gifts Are for Today

This book is addressed primarily to those who have already accepted that supernatural gifts are still available to believers today. However, we need to be ready to answer those who have questions or wish to raise challenges. Wayne Grudem is the author of perhaps the best-selling systematic theology in America.[67] Grudem is also the editor of one of the best surveys on the various positions related to miraculous gifts.[68] Grudem himself is interesting because his spiritual journey includes a period of time in association with the Vineyard Church, which has a heavy emphasis on spiritual gifts, and afterward, he settled into a Southern Baptist church.[69] He explains that there are many different positions on the question of "Are miraculous gifts for today?" but he synthesizes them into four groups: cessationists, open but cautious, third wave, and Pentecostal/Charismatic.[70] Each of these represents some variation of cessationism or continuation, but the variety recognizes that one can be open on some issues and not on others.

Cessationism

Cessationism is the belief that supernatural gifts, which are sometimes referred to as sign gifts, ceased at the end of the first century. Most cessationists do not attempt to prove their position based on explicit biblical texts but rather on inferences and patterns. It is a systematic approach to theology. The two texts that often come into play are 1 Cor. 13:10 and Eph. 4:13.

> As for prophecies, they will pass away; as for tongues, they will cease; as for knowledge, it will pass away. For we know in part, and we prophesy in part, but when the perfect comes, the partial will pass away. 1 Cor. 13:8–10 ESV

> And he gave the apostles, the prophets, the evangelists, the shepherds, and teachers, to equip the saints for the work of ministry, for building up the body of Christ, until we all attain to the unity of the faith and of the knowledge of the Son of God, to mature manhood, to the measure of the stature of the fullness of Christ, so that we may no longer be children, tossed to and fro by the waves and carried about by every wind of doctrine, by human cunning, by craftiness in deceitful schemes. Eph. 4:13 ESV

The Corinthian passage is the oldest approach in attempting to base cessationism directly on a biblical text. The argument is that supernatural gifts, especially tongues and prophecy, would remain until "that which is perfect is come," and then we will know all things, so that we no longer need these special gifts. According to this argument, the "perfect" refers to the Bible. Although it is difficult to find any major scholar who still holds to this view, it was a major argument of cessationists in past decades. There are at least two major objections to this interpretation. First, the canon of Scripture was not completed (or recognized as completed) until the fourth century. Most cessationists are not willing to admit that the supernatural gifts, including apostles, continued until this late date. The second objection is that knowledge is included in the list of things that will pass away. It is difficult to understand in what sense knowledge passed away with the completion of Scripture.

Supernatural Gifts Are for Today

Richard Gaffin bases his cessation position more on Ephesians 4:13, but he also relates it to 1 Corinthians 13:10.[71] Gaffin recognizes, as do most modern translations, that the Greek word *teleios* (translated "perfect") is better translated as "complete" or "mature."[72] It is the same word Jesus used when he said, "You, therefore, must be perfect, as your heavenly Father is perfect" (Matt. 5:48). Comparing 1 Corinthians 13:10 and Ephesians 4:13, Gaffin concludes that both passages refer to a temporary period of time in which the church is being established and comes to maturity. Thus, for Griffin, we cannot set a specific date or historic event for the passing away of the supernatural charismata. He strengthens his argument by saying that most people do not believe that apostles still exist today.[73] Therefore, the fact that (in his view) apostles ceased to exist after the foundation of the church, so did the other supernatural gifts.

Systematic theology does not require a proof text for each proposition. It is enough to draw on textual inferences interpreted by logic and history. B. B. Warfield was the author of one of the classical works on cessationism entitled *Counterfeit Miracles*.[74] Warfield's primary argument is that the gift of the Holy Spirit, with supernatural power, was bestowed exclusively by the laying on of hands by the apostles. "It could not be more emphatically stated that the Holy Ghost was conferred by the laying on of the hands, specifically of the Apostles, and of the Apostles alone."[75] Warfield states that only the initial outpouring on the Day of Pentecost and the outpouring at the home of Cornelius (Acts 10) occurred without the laying on of hands by apostles. He, therefore, concludes that this was the exclusive, or at least the normative, manner in which gifts were received by individuals, and thus, when the last apostle died, such gifts could no longer be distributed. Warfield also articulated the argument, which has become standard for cessationism, that the biblical miracles were clustered around certain periods and were not uniformly distributed. He writes, "Miracles do not appear on the page of Scripture vagrantly, here, there, and elsewhere indifferently, without assignable reason. They belong to revelation periods and appear only when God is speaking to His people through accredited messengers, declaring His gracious purposes."[76] Warfield and Gaffin refer to these time periods as "revelation periods," and Gaffin argues that miracles are "tethered" to such time periods.[77] Warfield and Gaffin are not saying that miracles only occurred during these limited time periods or epochs, only that miracles were rare outside such epochs. From that observation of the Old Testament, they argue that the apostolic age was a unique epoch or revelation period, and the miracles were not intended to be normative from that point forward. Robert Rothwell explains it this way:

> That the Holy Spirit is working today, however, does not have to mean that He continues to grant the charismatic gifts of tongues, prophecy, and healing today. These gifts are associated with the giving of special revelation. As we look throughout the history of redemption in Scripture, we see that miracles, prophecy, and ecstatic utterances such as tongues were not everyday occurrences but rather were associated with particular epochs. The era of Moses when the law was being given, the era of the old covenant prophets as instituted in the ministries of Elijah and Elisha, and the era of Jesus and the early Apostles that inaugurated the new covenant—these are the periods in biblical history when we see what we call the charismatic gifts manifested. In each of these eras, new special revelation was being given and the supernatural signs accompanied the deliverance of this revelation in order to authenticate it as from God. However, we know now that special revelation has ceased.[78]

The weakness of this argument is that it assumes that special revelation was the only purpose for miraculous gifts. It ignores biblical texts, such as Ephesians 4:11, that declare supernatural gifts are given for the upbuilding of the church until we all come to unity in the faith. When defining the epochs of special revelation, this theory fails to take seriously Joel's prophecy that dreams, visions, and prophecies will occur in the last days (Joel 2:28–32; Acts 2:17–21). There is no basis for saying that the "last days" ended two thousand years before the return of Christ—we are still living in the last days. While systematic theology (based on arguments from patterns, logic, and sometimes from silence) has always been used by the church as a valuable tool for interpreting Scripture, it can also lead to erroneous results. Conclusions drawn from patterns with only a few data points can never be conclusive. Gaffin admits, "The greatest danger for my position [cessationism] is . . . that we violate 'Do not go beyond what is written,'"(1 Cor. 4:6), as that principle applies in the church today."[79] As conservatives, we try to stick with the clear meaning of Scripture; cessationism is not clearly taught in Scripture; it is a conclusion that attempts to reconcile Scripture with the experience of the church. We should be asking the question "If we do not see the same types of miracles today as were experienced in the Book of Acts, why not?"

Middle of the Road

Within the cessationist ranks, there are those who are open to the possibility of miraculous gifts, but they approach the subject with skepticism and very little expectation of anything supernatural. Robert Saucy writes,

> To state my opinion up front, the New Testament does not explicitly teach the cessation of certain gifts at a particular point in the experience of the church. It is, therefore, impossible to say, on the basis of biblical teaching, that certain gifts cannot occur at any given time according to God's sovereign purpose. On the other hand, there are several lines of evidence that demonstrate that the miraculous phenomena experienced in the early biblical church are not standard for the life of the church throughout all time.[80]

From this starting point, Saucy moves quickly to Warfield's thesis that biblical miracles tend to be clustered around certain periods of time and were never intended to be normative.

John Piper represents a middle-of-the-road position that is more favorable than that of Saucy. Piper opened a blog post with these words:

> I am one of those Baptist General Conference people who believe that "signs and wonders" and all the spiritual gifts of 1 Corinthians 12:8–10 are valid for today and should be "earnestly desired" (1 Corinthians 14:1) for the edification of the church and the spread of the Gospel. I agree with the words of Martyn Lloyd-Jones, preached in 1965: "It is perfectly clear that in New Testament times, the gospel was authenticated in this way by signs, wonders, and miracles of various characters and descriptions. . . . Was it only meant to be true of the early church? . . . The Scriptures never anywhere say that these things were only temporary—never! There is no such statement anywhere."
>
> [Piper continues]
>
> I want to argue in this section that the New Testament teaches that spiritual gifts (including the more obviously supernatural or revelatory ones like prophecy and tongues) will continue until Jesus comes. The use of such gifts (miracles, faith, healings, prophecy, etc.) gives rise to what may sometimes be called "signs and wonders." Therefore, signs and wonders are part of the blessing we should pray for today.[81]

Supernatural Gifts Are for Today

Piper is very close to the Charismatic position even though he does not identify himself as Charismatic, and he does not profess to have any of the so-called sign gifts, nor does his church emphasize such gifts. However, Piper has the gifts of preaching and teaching, and he exercises the gifts with great power. He states: "There is no text in the New Testament that teaches the cessation of these gifts. But more important than this silence is the text that explicitly teaches their continuance until Jesus comes: namely, 1 Corinthians 13:8–12." Piper interprets "until that which is perfect comes" to mean the return of Christ. He then emphasizes 1 Corinthians 12:31: "Earnestly desire the higher gifts." Piper says we are being disobedient if we fail to seek spiritual gifts. He is very close to the Charismatic position.

Pentecostal, Charismatic, and Third Wave

Peter Wagner coined the term *third wave* to describe a movement of the Spirit that began in the early 1980s.[82] Wagner was a career missionary prior to becoming a full-time professor at Fuller Seminary's School of World Missions. In the latter years of his missionary service, he observed a fresh wave of miracles occurring on the mission field—more than he had observed in his early years.[83] After he joined the faculty at Fuller, he taught courses on evangelism and church growth, and his curriculum included studies on the impact of miracles on church growth. This work led hm to the observation that the church was experiencing a new movement of the Spirit. Wagner labeled the Pentecostal outpouring that began circa 1900 as the first wave, the Charismatic revival that began circa 1960 as the second wave, and a new movement that he identified circa 1980 as the third wave. As a practicing missionary at the beginning of the third wave, Wagner found the new wave to have a special emphasis on physical healing—more specifically, healing as a result of demonic deliverance.[84]

These three groups (Pentecostal, Charismatic, and third wave) have in common that they believe the supernatural gifts of the Spirit still occur in the church today. The main difference between the three is how they see the relationship between Baptism in the Spirit and spiritual gifts. Classical Pentecostals, at least in the early days of the movement, believed that you must be baptized in the Spirit as a second experience following salvation before you could have spiritual gifts— in effect, they did not believe that you had the Spirit in your life until you were baptized subsequent to salvation. Spirit baptism was considered the "gateway" to spiritual gifts.[85] The Charismatic movement, which began in the early 1960s, was more diverse in perspective. The Charismatic renewal began in many mainline churches, including Anglican, Methodist, and Catholic. The emphasis was on a renewal experience of the fullness of the Spirit, with the idea that the Holy Spirit was awakening, filling, and stirring the people of God. This filling of the Spirit was sometimes called Baptism in the Spirit and sometimes filled with the Spirit, but for most people, it was a continuation of what occurred during the new birth experience; it was not a one-time baptism that occurred after salvation. Many Charismatics remained in their denominational churches or joined Charismatic churches, but they did not consider themselves Pentecostal. The primary difference is that Charismatics generally do not agree with the two Pentecostal doctrines of subsequence and initial evidence. Subsequence means that Spirit baptism is a one-time event that occurs after conversion, and initial evidence is that speaking in tongues is the necessary evidence that one has received the baptism in the Spirit. Charismatics generally continue to hold their core beliefs, such as Wesleyan, Reformed, Presbyterian, Catholic, et cetera.

References to the waves of the Spirit in the twentieth century do not mean that there were no Charismatic experiences prior to this period. The work of the Spirit through spiritual outpourings and charismatic gifts has occurred throughout history. Such notable figures as St. Irenaeus (120-200), St. Anthony (251-136), St. Augustine (354-430), John Wesley (1703-1791), Charles Finney (1792-1875), and Edward Irving (1792-1834) reported miracles and similar experiences. Wesley was of the opinion that the charismatic gifts fell into disuse

Supernatural Gifts Are for Today

after Constantine declared Christianity the official state religion and religion became more formalized. Still, the charismatic gifts never ceased, they were simply less frequent.[86]

With this background, we can summarize the basic foundations of the teaching that miraculous gifts are still available to the church today. First, there are no biblical texts that state supernatural gifts, or sign gifts, would be withdrawn from the church after the apostolic age. Arguments can be made from 1 Corinthians 13:8–10: "When that which is perfect is come," prophecies will fail, and tongues will cease, but it is very inconclusive to argue that it is a reference to the completion of the Bible. Anthony Thiselton is correct when he states that 1 Corinthians 13:8–10 does not shed any light on the cessationist argument one way or another.[87] The second argument from the Scriptures is based on Ephesians 4:13 and argues that apostles have ceased to exist, and therefore, there must be an admission that at least some gifts have ceased; if the gift of apostle has ceased, perhaps others have ceased as well.[88] There are two counterarguments. First, the New Testament identifies various levels of apostles. The twelve apostles were eyewitnesses to the life and resurrection of Christ, but there were other apostles of lower rank who were not eyewitnesses. There is no indication that Ephesians 4:11 refers only to the twelve. Paul gives no indication that he expected the ministry of apostleship to disappear from the church with the passing of the twelve. The second response is that the ministry offices described in Ephesians 4:11 are not single gifts as described in 1 Corinthians 12. The ministry offices represent collections or groups of gifts that come together to support a ministry calling. Even if the ministry of apostleship were to pass away, it does not indicate that the individual gifts that make up that calling must necessarily cease.

The second strong argument for the continuation of supernatural miracles is that the church needs God's miraculous presence, and he designed the church to include this. Paul's letters, especially 1 Corinthians, Romans, and Ephesians, are the only material we have concerning spiritual gifts in the church. If Paul knew such gifts were temporary, it seems highly likely that he would have given instructions to the church regarding how the church should operate after the cessation of such gifts. The fact is that Paul described the New Testament church with the inclusion of supernatural gifts, and he gave no guidelines for how the church would operate without such gifts. The ministry callings listed in Ephesians 4 are given:

> For the equipping of the saints for the work of
> ministry, for the edifying of the body of Christ, till we
> all come to the unity of the faith and of the
> knowledge of the Son of God, to a perfect man. Eph.
> 4:12–13

Unless we want to argue that the church has reached full maturity and unity, we must acknowledge that we still need God's supernatural presence. Many cessationists argue that they still believe in miracles, but they don't believe in miraculous gifts appropriated to individuals.[89]

Third, I want to address the argument that the primary purpose of miracles is to accredit the apostles and thereby set the foundation for the new church. Specifically, I want to demonstrate that accrediting God's messengers and their message is certainly one purpose for miracles; it is not the only purpose. Some of the additional purposes for miracles include:

Miracles as demonstrations of God's power and his sovereignty. Someone might argue that the purpose of these miracles is to accredit God himself, but there can be no argument to limit such miracles to the apostolic age. When God orchestrated the release of the Israelites from Egypt, he began by arranging the ten plagues to demonstrate both his supreme power and his approval of Moses. The Egyptians were polytheists; they needed no proof of the existence of gods. The plagues demonstrated that the god of the Israelites was superior to the Egyptian gods. The Egyptians were able to duplicate the first two plagues but were unable to produce the plagues that followed (Ex. 7–8). The final demonstration of God's power in this scenario occurred as they crossed the Red Sea. God said to Moses, "I will get glory over

Supernatural Gifts Are for Today

Pharaoh and all his host, his chariots, and his horsemen. And the Egyptians shall know that I am the Lord, when I have gotten glory over Pharaoh, his chariots, and his horsemen" (Ex. 14:17–18). Latourelle speaks of "liberation miracles" as a type that both liberates people from sickness and bondage and displays God's compassion and his power.[90] When Jesus healed a demoniac who was blind and mute, the Pharisees muttered that he cast out demons by the power of Beelzebub. Jesus responded,

> If I cast out demons by Beelzebub, by whom do your sons cast them out? Therefore, they will be your judges. But if it is by the Spirit of God that I cast out demons, then the kingdom of God has come upon you. Matt. 12:22–28

The deliverance from demonism sets people free from bondage and also displays Jesus' power over the demons. Jesus' mission statement included, "He has sent me to proclaim liberty to the captives" (Lk. 4:18). Who can argue that such miracles are no longer needed?

Miracles as a demonstration of God's compassion. Jesus often preceded his miracles by expressing compassion for people's needs. What argument can be made that miracles of compassion are no longer needed? Examples of his compassion are numerous. Matthew tells us, "When he went ashore, he saw a great crowd, and he had compassion on them and healed their sick" (Matt. 14:14). The feeding of the four thousand was compassion based.

> Then Jesus called his disciples to him and said, "I have compassion on the crowd because they have been with me now three days and have nothing to eat. And I am unwilling to send them away hungry, lest they faint on the way." Matthew 15:32

When Jesus saw a funeral procession, he had compassion for the mother, who was also a widow.

> And when the Lord saw her, he had compassion on her and said to her, "Do not weep." Then he came up and touched the bier, and the bearers stood still. And he said, "Young man, I say to you, arise." And the dead man sat up and began to speak, and Jesus gave him to his mother. Lk. 7:13–17

Miracles in response to faith and prayer. Among the many purposes or functions of miracles, we also see that God sometimes performs miracles in response to the prayer of faith. Latourelle points out that in a great many miracles, Christ is the initiator, but

> Other miracles, however, are responses of Christ to petitions that are sometimes expressed in so many words, sometimes tacitly implied in a gesture or action. The blind men at Jericho asked that their eyes be opened (Mt 20:29–34); The Canaanite woman wins the desired healing by her persistence (Mt 15:21–28); the leper falls on his knees and implores Jesus (Mk 1:40–41); the centurion (Lk 7:3); Jairus (Lk 8:40); the father of the epileptic boy (Lk. 9:38–42).

We are challenged to provide a proper interpretation of Jesus' words, such as "Very truly I tell you, my Father will give you whatever you ask in my name" (Jn. 16:23); despite the challenge, such promises must have some meaning. Jesus' parable concerning the persistent widow and the unjust judge has hermeneutical challenges but must be given some weight. God will hear the cry of those who "cry out to him day and night" (Lk. 18:1–8).

Apostles and Prophets

Until the third wave, there was near unanimous consent that the ministry of apostleship ceased after the first century, and most Pentecostals and Charismatics accepted this view of the office of apostle. This belief is based on the idea that all apostles must be

Supernatural Gifts Are for Today

eyewitnesses of Jesus' life and resurrection. However, this view fails to recognize that there were various ranks and levels of authority among the New Testament apostles. The primary meaning of the word *apostle* (*apostolos*) is "sent one." It can also be translated as "missionary," "messenger," or "ambassador."[91] Apostles were often appointed in commerce as representatives of the company or business owner. Sometimes the word *apostle* was applied to a fleet of ships as they went out to represent a country or a wealthy enterprise.[92] The granting of the commission would define the mission and level of authority of the apostles being sent, and not every apostle had the same level of authority. It is clear that the original twelve apostles commissioned by Jesus had the same mission and level of authority; they were in a class by themselves. However, the early church recognized other apostles (sent ones, representatives, messengers) who had less authority than the twelve. Even after Jesus sent out an additional seventy-two apostles (Lk. 10:1), the original twelve continued to hold a special place of prominence. After Judas fell away, Peter found it necessary to preserve the cadre of twelve. The qualifications Peter set for this position are as follows:

> Therefore, it is necessary to choose one of the men who have been with us the whole time the Lord Jesus was living among us, beginning from John's baptism to the time when Jesus was taken up from us. For one of these must become a witness with us of his resurrection. Acts 1:21–22

The apostles chose Matthias to fill this position. However, many have argued that Paul was actually God's choice for the position. It should be noted, however, that Paul did not meet all the requirements. He did not accompany Jesus from the time of his baptism onward throughout his earthly ministry. Paul was certainly an apostle of great power and authority, but he was not one of the twelve. There is near-unanimous consent that Paul considered Barnabas an apostle.[93] Barnabas' commission was given in Acts 13:2–3, and in Acts 14:4, he and Paul are referred to as "the apostles." Others accepted as apostles include James the Lord's brother (Gal. 1:19), Andronicus, and Junias (Rom. 16:7). Epaphroditus is called an *apostolos* in Philippians 2:25, although most versions translate it as "messenger" because he was appointed by a local church, and his commission was not necessarily recognized by other churches. From this, we can affirm that there were different levels or classes of apostles and different methods of appointment. Matthias was chosen based on the casting of lots (the toss of a coin)

(Acts 1:26).

The point of all that we have written above is to show that in addition to the twelve, there were other apostles in the New Testament church. When Paul describes the fivefold ministry in Ephesians 4:11, he did not limit the office of an apostle to the original twelve. Clinton Arnold is correct when he states:

> The "apostles" he mentions here likely extend beyond the Twelve and Paul to include others whom the Lord Jesus has called to go, establish churches, and ground these new believers in the common faith. Their authority would be differentiated from the Twelve and Paul, who had "seen the Lord" (1 Cor. 9:1; Acts 1:21–22). Nevertheless, they are authorized by the risen Lord Jesus himself, who has called them to this role, and by the authoritative message of the gospel itself, which is imparted. Their function is closely tied up with their name, "one who is sent." . . . The church continues the mission of Jesus and the Twelve when the sovereign lord commissions and empowers individuals to go and proclaim the good news, establish churches, and teach them to observe all that the Lord commands (Matt. 28:19–20).[94]

In contrast, Douglas Moo argues that Paul's intent in Ephesians 4 is that the apostles and prophets would be replaced by the evangelists, pastors, and teachers—but his argument lacks any exegetical support.[95] He defines apostles as "the specially chosen men who had seen Christ and who had the authority to establish new-covenant norms."[96] Moo is correct in his definition of the twelve apostles, but he fails to recognize the various other classes of apostles.

Prophets are similar to apostles in that they minister under a commission from God, and they have limited authority. Paul states, "If your gift is prophesying, then prophesy in accordance with your faith" (Rom. 12:6). When Aaron and Miriam spoke against Moses, God said to them,

> When there is a prophet among you, I, the Lord, reveal myself to them in visions, I speak to them in dreams. But this is not true of my servant Moses; he is faithful in all my house. With him, I speak face to face, clearly and not in riddles. Num. 12:6–8

Clearly, not every prophet has the same level of communication with God. Just as not every apostle is commissioned to write Scripture, not every prophet's words are considered infallible—no more so than any other person in the exercise of a spiritual gift. Every spiritual gift is a manifestation of the Spirit (1 Cor. 12:7), but it flows through human channels. There are two great errors often made in this regard. The first error is to hold that everything is controlled by God with no human influence. That has never been the case, even with apostles and prophets. Paul and Barnabas argued (Acts 15:36–39), and Paul argued with Peter (Gal. 2:11). Paul was not omniscient; he did not know everything at all times (Acts 16:6–10). There were prophets in the church at Antioch, but their prophecies were not of the level to be included in Scripture (Acts 11:27).

Words of Caution about Apostles and Prophets

There is a growing emphasis today on the fivefold ministry as depicted in Ephesians 4. Along with the emphasis, there is a tendency to redefine the role of apostles in a way that humanizes their ministries in an unhealthy way. To be sure, an apostle is fully human in every way. However, when operating in the apostolic role, there must be a clear sense—observable to others—that the Holy Spirit is actively at work producing supernatural results. When Paul defended himself against those who criticized his ministry, he wrote, "I persevered in demonstrating among you the marks of a true apostle, including signs, wonders and miracles" (2 Cor. 12:12). Paul does not give a full list of the signs of an apostle; he simply says, "including signs, wonders, and miracles." In 2 Corinthians 11:23–23, Paul defended his apostleship by referring to how much he suffered for the gospel. The signs and miracles were not the substance of his ministry, but they affirmed God's calling on his life. Anyone who claims to be an apostle should have demonstrations of God's power that prove God is at work through the person's life. That is not to say that every apostle must be a miracle worker. As we stated above, there are different levels and ranks of apostles; but for any true apostle of any rank, there must be evidence of God at work.

Gift tests are sometimes given to entire congregations so each person may be aware of their place in the church. Too often, these tests are used to indicate that every person in the church is called into one of these five ministries. Every believer should have one or more gifts, but that does not mean every believer is called to one of the five ministries listed in Ephesians 4. In order to fit people into these five categories, the descriptions are often changed to make them less supernatural. For example, one of the most widely used tests for the fivefold ministry describes the gift (or office) of apostle this way:

> People who score highest with an Apostolic position are Dream Awakeners in the Kingdom of God. They awaken people to their God-designed potential. They are instrumental in people discovering who they really are and walking alongside them to get there. They forge new paths in the Kingdom and are a catalyst for change wherever they go.[97]

Supernatural Gifts Are for Today

The description does not require any supernatural manifestations or results—what Paul called "the marks of an apostle" (2 Cor. 12:12). Others simply describe an apostle in this way: "The spiritual gift of Apostle is the God-given ability to pioneer new churches in unchartered territories and mentor others to do the same."[98] When a gift test is used to help people decide where they fit into the fivefold ministry, the test will never say, "Sorry, you do not fit any one of these five, but you are still valued"; it will always lead the person to believe they are either an apostle, prophet, evangelist, pastor, or teacher. A person who is good at leadership and wants to start new organizations or projects will be identified as an apostle. A person who cares deeply about nurturing people will be identified as a pastor. The tests do not take into consideration the spirituality of the person. It is very doubtful that the early church would have recognized someone as an apostle simply because they planted a church, nor would they recognize someone as a prophet simply based on the fact that the person frequently speaks out on social issues.

I want to be clear that I do believe we could still have apostles and prophets in the church today. My argument is that an apostle is not simply a person who is good at leadership or planting new churches. The essence of apostleship is that the Holy Spirit anoints the person with power and enables them to do extraordinary things to build and advance the kingdom of God beyond the local church. The results of the apostle's ministry should clearly show that God is at work supernaturally. The same is true for the ministry of the prophet. The gift list in 1 Corinthians 12 is focused on individual gifts. The list in Ephesians 4 involves ministries or groups of gifts that work together. Some call the five ministries in Ephesians 4 "ministry offices," but others object that the early church, at the time of Paul's writing, did not have official positions. That distinction is probably not important. The first-century church did recognize apostles, bishops, and deacons, so there is no reason to object to other ministry offices.

Prophecy is one of the hallmarks of Charismatic experience. In Joel's prophecy concerning the last days (the prophecy was repeated by Peter on the Day of Pentecost), God states, "I will pour out my Spirit on all people. Your sons and daughters will prophesy, your old men will dream dreams, your young men will see visions" (Joel 2:28; Acts 2:17–18). God did not promise that people would receive gifts of healing or miracles—but they would prophesy. The verbal gifts of prophecy, tongues, and interpretation are distinctly related to the dispensation of the Spirit. As wonderful as this is, prophecy has caused the downfall of many people and churches. What are we to do about this fact? Paul responds, "Therefore, my brothers and sisters, be eager to prophesy, and do not forbid speaking in tongues. But everything should be done in a fitting and orderly way" (1 Cor. 14:39–40).

Not everyone who speaks a false word is intentionally a false prophet. Many well-meaning people speak from their own human spirit and mistake this for a word from God. Everything from business deals to marriage proposals has been given forth as prophecies. Prophesying the outcome of political elections has become particularly problematic. The 2020 US presidential election serves as a prime example. Several dozen Christian leaders prophesied that Donald Trump would win the election. When that did not happen, a few of those who prophesied were willing to admit their error, but some continued to insist that their prophecies were accurate and, in heaven, God still considers Mr. Trump to be the president.[99] The "prophets" were criticized by both Christian and secular media.[100] Craig Keener, himself a Charismatic, wrote in *Christianity Today*,

> The failed prophecies of Donald Trump's reelection may have damaged the credibility of the US independent Charismatic wing of evangelicalism more than any event since the televangelist scandals of the 1980s. They have led some outsiders to criticize Christianity itself and rightly call us to introspection."[101]

Paul's instruction to the church at Corinth is very interesting and enlightening.

> Two or three prophets should speak, and the others should evaluate what is said. And if someone sitting down receives a revelation, the person who is speaking should conclude. For you can all prophesy one after another, so all can learn and be encouraged.
> 1 Cor. 14:29–31 NET

Paul instructs the spiritual leaders of the congregation to evaluate (judge, KJV) what the prophets are saying. Paul would not say whether he assumed all the prophets in the local church were infallible. In his instructions to the church at Rome, he writes, "And we have different gifts according to the grace given to us. If the gift is prophecy, that individual must use it in proportion to his faith" (Rom. 12:6 NET). Again, he acknowledges that the prophets may have different levels of maturity, and he warns them not to prophecy beyond their level of grace and faith. The Corinthian passage also assumes there will be multiple prophets in the local church, as there were at the church in Jerusalem (Acts 11:27). If one person is prophesying and another also has a revelation, the first is to keep their message brief so that the other prophets have time to deliver their messages (1 Cor. 14:30). This makes it clear that prophecy is not an ecstatic utterance that takes the speaker into a trance beyond their control.

Church leaders are instructed to evaluate the prophecies. In the Old Testament, false prophets who encouraged rebellion against the Lord were put to death (Deut. 13:5). This does not mean that every prophet who uttered a false word was put to death, but only those who knowingly spoke against God. Paul's instruction to the Romans and the Corinthians assumes the possibility that a genuine believer may mistakenly speak an untruth. He instructs the other elders to evaluate and discern prophecies to protect the flock and take corrective action where required. When a person uses their gift in a disruptive manner—whether the gift is prophecy, tongues, or any other gift—the elders must take corrective action. The brother or sister should receive additional teaching and guidance and should be restricted from exercising that gift publicly until the elders are confident the person has learned to use their gift responsibly.

Summary

Charismatics believe that all the gifts described in the New Testament are available to all believers today, and God distributes them according to his sovereign will. Most non-Charismatics (often called cessationists) believe that most supernatural gifts (often called sign gifts) ceased to exist after the end of the first century. Charismatics, on the other hand, find that God is still at work in supernatural ways, and we appeal to the fact that Scripture does not state or even hint that supernatural gifts will end. Charismatics also argue that the New Testament describes the way God builds and functions in the church, and the biblical description of the church includes miraculous gifts. Without such gifts, a church today would not represent the church described in the New Testament.

God builds the church through miraculous gifts, and he invites his people to participate in his work. God could do his work without humans, but he has always chosen to include them. The Old Testament prophets, judges, and kings were God's appointed messengers to speak his words and lead the people. In a similar fashion, God distributes spiritual gifts to believers in the body of Christ today. The gifts are not just for a few people who have a special calling to ministry; they are for every believer. Some believers have not discovered or developed their spiritual gift(s), but the normal pattern for the church is that every believer should have one or more gifts, and they should be participants in the work of God as God enables them. One of the primary purposes of spiritual gifts is to:

> Equip his people for works of service, so that the body of Christ may be built up until we all reach unity in the faith and in the knowledge of the Son of God and become mature, attaining to the whole measure of the fullness of Christ. Eph. 4:12–13

Supernatural Gifts Are for Today

This is an ongoing need in the church, and the church will be deficient unless God's people, empowered by the Spirit, use their gifts to build up others and strengthen the church.

We do not wish to disparage those who hold different views from the view presented in this book. God calls us to peace and unity as much as possible. Holiness, as presented in Chapters 7 and 9, includes humility and grace in our relationships with others.

Chapter 5
The Power of Faith

> "Take heart, daughter," he said, "your faith has healed you." And the woman was healed at that moment. Matt. 9:22

> Then he touched their eyes and said, "According to your faith, let it be done to you." Matt. 9:29

> And he did not do many miracles there because of their lack of faith. Matt. 13:58

The relationship between faith and miracles is confirmed throughout Scripture. The Word of Faith movement claims that you can have anything you desire if you have enough faith. (Of course, they exclude things that are clearly outside God's will.) Kenneth Hagin writes,

> [Commenting on Rom. 10:8–10]
>
> This passage in Romans deals specifically with salvation. But we receive salvation from God in the same way we receive other provisions from God. Every other provision was included in that salvation. Through His death, burial, and resurrection, Jesus

The Power of Faith

> made salvation, preservation, healing, provision, wholeness, and every good thing to us. Jesus did the work. How do we receive those provisions? With our heart we believe it, with our mouth we confess it, and then we receive it.
>
> [Commenting on Matt. 21:21–22.]
>
> Notice verse 22 says: "And all things, whatsoever ye shall ask in prayer, believing, ye shall receive." How many things? All things. "All things" includes healing! Also, this passage in Matthew bears witness with our passage in Romans 10—believe, ask (or say), and receive.[102]

The Word of Faith movement holds that if you pray and do not receive the answer, in the majority of cases, it is because of a lack of faith. You should believe you have received the answer even if the answer does not yet appear. In reaction to this teaching, many Christians say we should never tell a person who is not healed that it is because of a lack of faith. I agree we don't want to make a sick person feel even worse by "blaming" them, but we should be as honest as possible. When Jesus was in his hometown of Nazareth, Matthew tells us that he "did not do many miracles there because of their unbelief" (Matt. 13:58). Mark says Jesus "could not" do many miracles (Mk. 6:5). Mark does not tell us if Jesus tried and failed, or if he knew it would not work so he didn't try; this latter interpretation is closer to Matthew's meaning. In any case, Jesus' ability or willingness to heal was limited by the faith of the people. We can also learn from the man healed at the Pool of Bethesda (Jn. 5:1–15). After Jesus healed the man, he said to him, "See, you are well again. Stop sinning, or something worse may happen to you" (Jn. 5:14). We can see that even after Jesus healed a person, the same illness or something worse could come back on them.

We will begin this chapter by exploring the impact of faith on answers to prayer. The greatest obstacle to faith is not knowing if it is God's will to answer the prayer. Chuck Swindoll states that it is rarely God's will to heal people.[103] God can heal, but he seldom does. Sickness is very often the result of original sin, and we are not yet delivered from the effects of this. In stark contrast, many Pentecostals—and some contemporary Charismatics—hold that healing is included in atonement and therefore guaranteed to everyone. Keith Warrington states that nearly 90 percent of Pentecostals believe healing is included in the atonement.[104] The late John Wimber, the founder of the Vineyard Association of Churches, writes, "Everything the devil introduced to men and women was undone by Jesus at the cross, which of course, includes sickness."[105] The belief that healing is included in the atonement is based on Scriptures such as Isaiah 53 and 1 Peter 2.

> But He was wounded for our transgressions, He was bruised for our iniquities; The chastisement for our peace was upon Him, And by His stripes we are healed. Isa. 53:5 NKJV

> He himself bore our sins in his body on the cross, so that we might die to sins and live for righteousness; by his wounds you have been healed. 1 Pet. 2:24

Although the biblical text relates healing to Christ's death and resurrection, most evangelicals do not regard healing as being included in the atonement because, they argue, whatever is in the atonement—like salvation—is available to everyone who asks for it, and it is 100 percent effective. Healing, on the other hand, seems to be of a different nature; not everyone is healed. There are also other effects of the Adamic fall that are not reversed in the atoning death of Christ.

The Power of Faith

Is it God's will for everyone to be healed? I wish to argue that in most cases, God does want to answer our prayers, including prayers for healing, but there will always be exceptions. Paul prayed three times to be healed from his thorn in the flesh (2 Cor. 12:7–10). Paul was not healed, but God did reveal the reason to him. We must admit there are times when God does not heal, and very often, we do not know the reason. However, if we are to believe Scripture, it is only by rare exception that God does not want to heal. If God wants to heal (and answer other prayers), why does it not happen? The majority of the times in Scripture, Jesus related it to lack of faith and, secondly, to sin. Jesus also related success in answers to prayer directly to faith. Consider the following three facts concerning faith.

1) Lack of faith prevents answers to prayer (Matt. 8:26, 13:58, 17:20).

2) Positive faith causes miracles to happen (Matt: 8:5–10, 9:2, 9:22, 9:29, 21:21; Mk. 5:34, 10:52; Lk. 17:6, 17:19, 18:42)

3) Sin can lead to sickness (Jn. 5:14; 1 Cor. 11:30).

While addressing the question of whether healing is in the atonement, it might be helpful to reconsider the meaning of atonement. The complexity of the issue is that the word *atonement* can have several different meanings, and it is used in the New Testament as a metaphor with different implications.[106] Since the Reformation, the predominate view of atonement is related to penal substitution: Christ died to pay the penalty for our sins. Wayne Grudem argues, "The justice of God also required that God find a way that the penalty due to us for our sins would be paid (for he could not accept us into fellowship with himself unless the penalty was paid)."[107] This view raises certain ethical issues concerning God. Why did God require a blood penalty? God is sovereign, and he makes the rules, so why does he have such a rule? Nevertheless, Luther and Calvin found this to be the best explanation for why Christ had to die. The penal substitution doctrine is based on the Old Testament view of blood sacrifices. A second concept found in the New Testament points to atonement as a "ransom" for sinners.

The primary verses used to support the ransom theory include "For even the Son of Man came not to be served but to serve, and to give his life as a ransom for many" (Mk. 10:45) and "Christ Jesus, who gave himself as a ransom for all" (1 Tim. 2:5–6). Just like penal substitution, the ransom perspective poses questions that are difficult to answer. For example, to whom was the ransom paid, and why? Irenaeus argued that the ransom was paid to the devil because sinful mankind sold himself into bondage to the devil. The counterargument is that the devil never owned anyone, so why would God pay a ransom to get back his own property? The third view of atonement is the spiritual warfare view, and it includes the fact that Christ won a victory over Satan through his death on the cross; Gustaf Aulén calls this the *Christus Victor* view of atonement.[108] According to Aulén, this was the predominate view of the church prior to the Reformation. He describes it as the idea of the Atonement as a divine conflict and victory; Christ—*Christus Victor*—fights against and triumphs over the evil powers of the world, the "tyrants" under which mankind is in bondage and suffering, and in Him, God reconciles the world to Himself.[109]

The *Christus Victor* could also be called the kingdom victory model. Christ won the victory over Satan, thus establishing a new phase of the kingdom of God. R. C. Sproul calls this "a cosmic victory of Jesus over Satan and his Kingdom. Passages like Hebrews 2:14 tell us that when Christ died on the cross, He destroyed the power of the evil one."[110] The kingdom has been described as "yet and not yet." The kingdom has come, and yet it is not fully victorious at this time. There remains a struggle (warfare) between the kingdom of God and the kingdom of Satan; Paul still calls Satan "the god of this world" (2 Cor. 4:4). The kingdom of God has been inaugurated but not fully consummated. In terms of healing, every attempt at doing so by faith is a matter of spiritual warfare—Satan stands in opposition. In summary, atonement can be seen as penal substitution, in which God paid the penalty for our sins. It is also referred to as ransom, in which

The Power of Faith

God paid for our redemption. And in the third biblical reference, atonement refers to God's kingdom victory over Satan.

If we view the atonement as cosmic warfare resulting in the establishing of the kingdom of God, we can conclude that healing is included in the atonement, but the kingdom is not yet fully victorious. The enemy is defeated but not vanquished. Thus, we conclude that atonement is a metaphor with different levels of meaning. Salvation is available to all and is 100 percent effective to all who call on the name of Jesus in faith. Healing is of a different nature; attempts to heal launch the parties into spiritual warfare in an environment where healing is desired but not guaranteed. Swindoll argues that if God wanted everyone healed, they would be healed because whatever God wants to happen always happens.[111] His argument fails to recognize that the people of God are locked in vicious combat, and there are victories, and there are temporary defeats. God wants everyone to be saved, but not everyone is saved.

Limitations on Faith

> He replied, "Because you have so little faith. Truly I tell you, if you have faith as small as a mustard seed, you can say to this mountain, 'Move from here to there,' and it will move. Nothing will be impossible for you." Matt. 17:20

> Then the LORD said to me: "Even if Moses and Samuel were to stand before me, my heart would not go out to this people. Send them away from my presence! Let them go! Jer. 15:1

"Nothing will be impossible for you" (Matt. 17:21) is a key verse for the Word of Faith movement. It is hard to argue against a literal interpretation of this verse except to say that experience, as well as biblical examples, forces us to interpret the text in accordance with reality. There are several reasons why prayer may not be answered, even if the person has strong faith.

Limitation 1: the will of God. No prayer can overcome the sovereignty of God. "Moving mountains" is a metaphor for doing that which is seemingly impossible. Jesus does not give anyone the actual ability to move literal mountains; if he did, the planet would be in chaos. God does not want us to destroy the planet for our own selfish or foolish reasons. God has a plan for mankind and for the earth, and we fit into that plan. God has left some things subject to our will and our actions, but somethings are firmly decided through God's sovereignty. From the time of Adam and Eve's sin, certain things have been set into motion that cannot be reversed until Jesus returns, destroys the current earth, and establishes a new heaven and a new earth (Isa. 65:17; Rev. 21:21).

There are times when God will listen to the prayer of faith and relent from what he had planned to do, but there are other cases when God's mind is set and will not change. God chose Saul to be the first king of Israel, but as a result of Saul's failures, God removed Saul and placed David on the throne. God said, concerning Saul, "I regret that I have made Saul king because he has turned away from me and has not carried out my instructions" (1 Sam. 15:11). When God said he would destroy the people of Nineveh, they repented, and God changed his plan (Jon. 3:10). We cannot always know God's plan for certain, but we should pray with faith until God shows us otherwise. Paul prayed three times for his thorn in the flesh to be removed. God did not remove the thorn, but he did reveal to Paul the reason the thorn was necessary. The parable of the persistent widow teaches us that we "should always pray and not give up" (Lk. 18:1–8). Paul prayed about the thorn until God revealed the answer.

Limitation 2: the will of other people. Many people have prayed for years for a spouse or a child to be saved—and we should keep on praying. However, we have no assurance of how that person will respond. God never saves a person against their will; that person must respond based on their own faith. Our prayer should be that God will soften their heart and give them saving faith. Saving faith grows out of receiving a new understanding of God and the plan of salvation. Saving faith requires more than cognitive knowledge; it requires faith that goes beyond head knowledge. God is the source of saving faith, but it requires some level of cooperation on the part of the recipient. Regardless of whether one is Calvinist or Armenian, salvation is not forced upon another person. We can pray for a person to be delivered from an addiction, but that person must cooperate by surrendering their desires and actions in order to be delivered and healed. We should continue to pray and ask God to bring them to a place of change, but we cannot force the issue no matter how much faith we exert.

Limitation 3: spiritual warfare. Without spiritual discernment, we cannot always know when a prayer is being resisted by spiritual forces. In most cases, if not all, a prayer for healing or for someone else's salvation will be met with spiritual resistance. When the disciples were unable to cast out a demon, Jesus answered that it was because of their lack of faith (Matt. 17:17–21, Mk. 9:29). In the disputed text, which is omitted from newer translations, Jesus added, "However, this kind does not go out except by prayer and fasting" (NKJ 17:21).[112] If we can learn from the text that was received by the church for centuries, Jesus is teaching that some demons are stronger than others. While Jesus had no problem casting out the strong demon, the apostles could not do so. Jesus said that additional prayer and fasting are necessary to drive out these stronger demons.

The Supernatural Aspect of Faith

Faith transcends the boundaries of earth and exceeds the laws of nature. David Hume argued that a miracle is, by his definition, an exception to the "laws of nature." He then argues that the laws of nature are so well established that there can be no exceptions; therefore, miracles are impossible by definition.[113] Faith recognizes that God is the author and creator of the laws of nature, and they remain under his control. The Roman centurion wanted Jesus to heal his servant. When Jesus offered to go to his home, the centurion replied:

> Lord, I do not deserve to have you come under my roof. But just say the word, and my servant will be healed. For I myself am a man under authority, with soldiers under me. I tell this one, "Go," and he goes; and that one, 'Come,' and he comes. I say to my servant, "Do this," and he does it. When Jesus heard this, he was amazed and said to those following him, "Truly I tell you, I have not found anyone in Israel with such great faith." Matt. 8:8–10

Jesus was amazed that this Roman centurion understood that he had power beyond the natural realm. He understood that Jesus could give orders, and spiritual forces would carry out those orders transcending the natural and physical realm.

The woman with the blood disease is recorded in all three Synoptics, but only Mark and Luke record Jesus' response:

> At once Jesus realized that power had gone out from him. He turned around in the crowd and asked, "Who touched my clothes?" "You see the people crowding against you," his disciples answered, "and yet you can ask, 'Who touched me?'" But Jesus kept looking around to see who had done it. Then the woman, knowing what had happened to her, came and fell at his feet and, trembling with fear, told him the whole truth. He said to her, "Daughter, your faith has healed you. Go in peace and be freed from your suffering." Mk. 5:30–34

> "Who touched me?" Jesus asked. When they all denied it, Peter said, "Master, the people are crowding and pressing against you." But Jesus said, "Someone

> touched me; I know that power has gone out from me." Lk 8:45–46

In both records, Jesus seemed surprised that power had gone out from him without him taking any action. It is apparent that the woman's touch of faith drew out the power and required no specific action on Jesus' part. This does not imply that the power was cosmological and not directly from Christ. Rather, it implies that the power of faith activates the power of God with no apparent requirement for God to consciously decide on the issue. Although this was while Jesus was still in human form, the principle remains instructive as to how faith works.

When Peter saw Jesus walking toward him on the water, he called out, "Lord, if it's you ... tell me to come to you on the water" (Matt. 14:28). We cannot take this to imply that everyone at all times can walk on water. In response to Peter's request, Jesus responded, "Come" (Matt. 14:29). Jesus had given Peter a specific acknowledgment that his request to walk on water would be granted. Some people have presumed beyond their level of faith or beyond any promise found in Scripture. The people of Jesus' day recognized that he was the Messiah because of the unusual miracles he performed (Acts 2:22). Other prophets and apostles performed miracles, but none of the magnitude that would lead to the conclusion that they were the Messiah. Jesus said we can "move mountains,"—but we know from the consistency of Scripture that our actions produced by faith are limited to the sovereignty of God.

Faith as a Lifestyle

> [5]. By faith Enoch was taken up so that he would not see death, and he was not found because God took him up; for before he was taken up, he was attested to have been pleasing to God. [6]. And without faith it is impossible to please Him, for the one who comes to God must believe that He exists, and that He proves to be One who rewards those who seek Him. [7]. By

> faith Noah, being warned by God about things not yet seen, in reverence prepared an ark for the salvation of his household, by which he condemned the world, and became an heir of the righteousness which is according to faith. [8]. By faith Abraham, when he was called, obeyed by going out to a place which he was to receive for an inheritance; and he left, not knowing where he was going.
>
> [23.] By faith Moses, when he was born, was hidden for three months by his parents, because they saw he was a beautiful child; and they were not afraid of the king's edict. [24]. By faith Moses, when he had grown up, refused to be called the son of Pharaoh's daughter, [25]. choosing rather to endure ill-treatment with the people of God than to enjoy the temporary pleasures of sin, [26]. considering the reproach of Christ greater riches than the treasures of Egypt; for he was looking to the reward. Heb. 11:5–26

Faith is not an instantaneous virtue that comes to the surface when a miracle is needed. Faith is a lifestyle that grows and develops over a period of time. That is why Jesus said, "This kind only goes out through prayer [and fasting]" (Mk. 9:29). Some translations have it that prayer drives out the stronger demons (NIV), but it seems likely that he is saying that prayer builds up one's faith to be prepared for such occasions. A life of prayer and faith prepares you in advance for when the need arises. When David, while still a young shepherd boy, heard Goliath taunting Israel's army, David said to Saul:

> Your servant has been keeping his father's sheep. When a lion or a bear came and carried off a sheep from the flock, I went after it, struck it and rescued the sheep from its mouth. When it turned on me, I seized it by its hair, struck it and killed it. Your

The Power of Faith

> servant has killed both the lion and the bear; this uncircumcised Philistine will be like one of them, because he has defied the armies of the living God. The Lord who rescued me from the paw of the lion and the paw of the bear will rescue me from the hand of this Philistine. Saul said to David, "Go, and the Lord be with you." 1 Sam. 17: 34–37

David's previous experiences prepared him for the day of battle. When facing enemies—whether demons or other types of enemies—that is no time to learn how to fight; the warrior must prepare in advance and grow strong and wise. In Acts 17, we read about the seven sons of Sceva who watched Paul cast out demons, and they tried to do the same by mimicking what Paul said to the demons. The spirits knew that these men did not have the power or experience to cast them out, and they turned on the young men and wreaked havoc on them. Faith, discernment, and wisdom grow over time, and they produce power. Power is not a standalone gift; it always comes packaged with wisdom and faith.

Summary

The very nature of Charismatic life and theology anticipates miracles. Furthermore, it anticipates that we, as the people of God, participate in those miracles both as beneficial recipients and as God's instruments in bringing them about. Faith has three aspects: first, it is belief in God's power and his willingness to perform miracles for his own glory and the benefit of his people. Second, faith is a lifestyle that anticipates the supernatural power of God breaking into the everyday lives of his people. Third, faith—after it has come to maturity—is the active ingredient that brings miracles into action (Mk. 5:30–34).

Without faith, it is impossible to please God (Heb. 11:6). Faith as a lifestyle is indispensable to the Christian walk. "We live by faith, not by sight" (2 Cor. 5:7). In Chapter 1, we described a Charismatic as "a Christian who has a deep awareness of the Holy Spirit's presence, and who believes that the Holy Spirit continues to work supernatural manifestations (supernatural gifts of the Spirit) through Christians today." The church at Corinth was a Charismatic church, and Paul testifies that they did not "lack any spiritual gift" (1 Cor. 1:7). Paul also wrote to the Ephesian church, saying, "Since we live by the Spirit, let us keep in step with the Spirit" (Eph. 5:25). We live by the Spirit and keep in step with the Spirit by living in faith. When faith becomes a lifestyle, we are prepared and equipped to exercise spiritual gifts and fight spiritual warfare when the need arises. Faith can "move mountains," which is a metaphor meaning faith can do that which seems impossible. All works of faith are empowered by God, but they are also limited by the sovereign will of God. The life of faith allows us to participate in the supernatural work of God. To walk in faith also means that we walk in awareness of the Spirit's presence, and we learn to know how God works and to be in alignment with his will. Faith is not just an action of the moment; it is a lifestyle.

Chapter 6
Spirit and Scripture

The Bible is the most tangible object we have that represents God. In the Old Testament, it was the Ark of the Covenant; in the current age, evangelicals revere the Bible as the visible representation of God's connection with mankind. We view the Bible as inerrant, and what it says about God, we believe to be true. In fact, many evangelicals hold that God speaks today only through Scripture. Charismatics, on the other hand, generally believe that God speaks in a multitude of different ways.

Charismatic theology reads the Bible not as history, but as God's living word through which he continues to speak inspired messages to the church and to individuals in every age of time. Within Charismatic theology, our primary concern is how the Holy Spirit delivers God's word to people today. There are many different methods of interpreting Scripture, but they can be broadly understood in two categories: static interpretations and dynamic interpretations. Properly speaking, these are the result of different hermeneutical methods; hermeneutics is the science of textual interpretation.

In the static view, God inspired the original text, and inspiration stops at that point. Preachers may use illustrations and metaphors to explain the meaning of the text, but this is not under the control of the Holy Spirit according to the static view. With the static view, inspiration happened in the past. Under the dynamic view, inspiration is a continuous process that never stops, and God continues to speak through the text. In the static view, a text can have only one meaning, and that meaning is the same at all times, in all places, and in all contexts. The meaning of the text can only be the literal meaning of the words, and no spiritual or theological meanings are acceptable. God has nothing to say except what has already been written. In the dynamic view, the Spirit may bring new truths to light that were not previously revealed to humankind. In the static view, the process of revelation has ended. In the dynamic view, God is always at work, revealing himself and his message to those who will listen.

In the static view, words always have the same meaning regardless of the text or context. The spirituality of the reader is not important. For example, Carl Henry argued that the Bible is a rational book and can be understood by any rational being—no spiritual assistance is required.[114] In the dynamic view, God speaks through the text to people who are alive in the Spirit. The dynamic view favors the words of Jesus: "Therefore every scribe who has been trained for the kingdom of heaven is like a master of a house, who brings out of his treasure what is new and what is old" (Matt. 13:52 ESV). The treasure is the Word of God, and those trained by the Spirit will continually bring out things new as well as things old. In the sections that follow, we will explore some of the more popular views of biblical interpretation today.

The Bible as History

The predominant method of biblical interpretation used among scholars today is the historical-critical method of interpretation.[115] This view sees the Bible as a history of God's people, what they believed, and how they lived in times past. N. T. Wright is probably the most prolific proponent of this view. He writes, "The study of Jesus is first and foremost a matter of history, needing careful ancillary use of literary study of the texts and theological study of implications."[116] The historical-critical method assumes that the most objective way to study the Bible is by determining the correct grammatical meaning of the words in the original context and as understood by the original audience. The result of the historical method is that we read the Bible as history rather than as God's living word. The historical method does not assume the Bible has any distinctly spiritual qualities that would make it any different from any other book. Wright argues that the Bible does not have "magical" powers.[117] Within academic circles, *magic* is a pejorative term referring to superstition rather than genuine divine power.

The historical-critical method has its roots in Enlightenment philosophy. The Enlightenment project began in the seventeenth century in Europe. The goal of the project was to explain everything in rational scientific terms and discard everything else as myths. Prior to this, the Bible was assumed to be true and went without question. Enlightenment-era philosophers believed that science holds all of the answers and that everything—including religion—must be measured by the test of scientific rationalism. Theologians faced the task of trying to gain professional credibility by reconciling faith and science. Several different models of interpretation came about as a result of this tension between science and faith. The primary strategy was to align religion with other fields of science. For example, various theologians describe religion as a type of anthropology, sociology, philosophy, or history. This, of course, requires that religion be evaluated by scientific methods—no supernatural evidence or presuppositions are allowed.

In Charismatic theology, we are concerned with how the Holy Spirit delivers God's word to people today. Reading the Bible as history does not ask or answer the question, "What is God saying to us today through this text?" The historian only wants to know "What did God say to the original audience," or, more likely, "What did the original audience believe that God was saying?" Charismatic theology can never separate the Word of God from the Spirit of God. The Bible becomes the Word of God as the Spirit speaks through the written word to the hearts and minds of people.

The Bible as a Legal Text

The Old Testament law was written very much as a legal text. Leviticus, Numbers, and Deuteronomy told the Israelites exactly how they were to live and worship, and there was no room for variance. Many people today read the entire Bible, including the New Testament, as a legal text. Every verse is examined for imperatives that can be stated as legal commands. Reading the Bible as a legal text does not recognize the different genres of Scripture and fails to bring out the richness of poetry, historical narratives, and symbolism. The wisdom literature (Proverbs, Job, Ecclesiastes, and Song of Solomon) is turned into legalistic commands rather than pearls of wisdom. Every genre of literature has its own method of interpretation. A book of poetry is read and understood in one way, a history book in another way, a math or science text in another way, and a legal text has its own method of understanding.

If we consider the Bible to be primarily a legal text, the precise legal definition of every word is of critical importance. Every sentence and every paragraph must be translatable into imperatives to be obeyed, or it has no value. However, Paul has already declared that we are no longer under the law (Rom. 6:14). The written law of the past is redefined and "written on our hearts" (Rom. 2:15). We might prefer to have everything written in black and white to remove all subjectivity from the process, but God chooses to lead by his Spirit and have his people walk by faith. God set us free from the law, and Paul warned us again and again against going back to legalism. Certainly, the Bible does have commands that are to be obeyed, but it is a serious error to treat the entire Bible, especially the New Testament, as a legal text. The purpose of the Bible is to allow God to speak to his people—not just as a historical record or as a legal document.

Paul tells us, "All Scripture is God-breathed and is useful for teaching, rebuking, correcting and training in righteousness" (2 Tim. 3:16). Charismatics read the entire Bible as a message from God that is applicable to our lives today. We understand we cannot take everything literally and apply it to ourselves, but God does have a message in the text as the Spirit brings out the application. However, for the Charismatic believer, the meaning of a biblical text is not limited to historical records of facts or the literal meaning of the words. The Bible is the "Living Word" of God, and the Spirit inspires the reading of the Word in new and fresh ways as he chooses. The wind (*pneuma*) of the Spirit is always active.

The Bible as a Spiritual Text

The Bible is the work of the Holy Spirit through human authors; thus, we have the doctrine of the dual authorship of Scripture. God was the primary author, and he was assisted by humans as the secondary authors. The balance between how much God controlled the process and how much the human authors were at liberty to reflect their own insights, memories, vocabulary, and theological understanding is debatable—but God used this process to produce a fully inspired Bible.

The concept of dual authorship means that two minds were involved in the process, and the two minds did not have equal knowledge or equal access to information. The historical method of interpretation focuses on the intent of the human author. Gordon Fee, in his wonderful book *How to Read The Bible*, asserts that authorial intent is one of the keys to interpreting what the Bible means.[118] Unfortunately, authorial intent usually only refers to the human author. If we really want to know the intent of the author, we must acknowledge that God is the primary author, and humans were the secondary authors. This does not mean that the human was a mere mechanical instrument; certainly, the human authors used their own thoughts, concerns, vocabularies, and theological understandings. For example, scholars have given considerable attention to the similarities and differences between the four gospels. It is assumed, based on textual comparisons, that Mark wrote his gospel first, and Matthew and Luke used Mark as a source document. There are other similarities between Matthew and Luke that cannot be traced to Mark, so we have introduced another source document called *quelle* (or Q for short; *quelle* is German for "source"). The Q document is entirely hypothetical because no one has ever found such a document, nor can we prove that it existed. The idea was invented as a possible way to explain the portions of Matthew and Luke that are almost identical but are lacking in Mark. Critical scholars cannot accept that the Holy Spirit gave the words to the human authors, so there must be a plausible explanation. The historical-grammatical approach assumes that everything can be explained through historical research with no appeal to the supernatural work of God. The task of biblical interpretation is to discover what the human author intended, and part of that research is to understand the author's sources.

Dual authorship accepts the fact that God the Holy Spirit inspired the human writers, and while permitting humans to explain things in their own words and their own vocabularies, God guided the process to ensure the accuracy of the text. Dual authorship assumes that God and man worked together, with both having a significant impact on the result. Within that process, it is certainly reasonable to assume that God had more foreknowledge and insight than did the human authors. Whatever understanding or insight the human authors may have had, God had his own insight and intentions. The knowledge of the apostle or prophet was limited to what God revealed to them, but God's knowledge far exceeds what was known to the human instrument. It is totally rational—both cognitively and spiritually—to understand that God may have included meanings within the text that the human author was not aware of, and that God might reveal these additional truths to readers at a later time. Jesus implied as much when he said to his disciples,

> Blessed are your eyes, because they see; and your ears, because they hear. For truly I say to you, that many prophets and righteous men desired to see what you see and did not see it; and to hear what you hear and did not hear it. Matt. 13:16–17

Spirit and Scripture

The task then of hermeneutics, or biblical interpretation, is to discover and interpret what God wants to say through the text, not limited to the literal meaning of the words or even the human author's intent. Prior to the Reformation, it was commonly understood that the Bible has multiple layers of meaning; at the very least, it has a literal meaning and a spiritual meaning. The principal Reformers (Luther, Calvin, et al.) denied that Scripture can have spiritual meanings aside from the literal meaning. They did so in order to combat what they saw as abuses by the Catholic Church in formulating doctrines without biblical basis. Prior to the Reformation, most theologians of the church were trained in the methods of Bible interpretation espoused by Origen and Augustine, which relied heavily on allegory to explain the spiritual meanings of the text. Luther did not simply reject the interpretive methods of the early church fathers; he also rejected the idea that Scripture can have a spiritual sense in addition to the literal sense. Several suggestions have been made regarding how we could hear the voice of the Spirit and still be faithful to the biblical text. In all cases, it requires that we accept the Bible as a living text, not merely a historical document.

Sensus Plenior: The Spiritual Meaning of the Text

Catholic scholar Raymond Brown's pioneering work on *sensus plenior* presents the view that a text may have multiple meanings.[119] *Sensus plenior* is a Latin term meaning "fuller meaning," but for the sake of simplicity, in this book, we will simply use the term *spiritual meaning* of the text. Brown argues that in addition to the literal meaning of the text, Scripture also contains a fuller meaning or spiritual meaning. In support of his argument, Brown cites how the New Testament authors quoted from the Old Testament—often adding meanings not apparent in the original text.

Sensus plenior includes three key elements: (1) the spiritual meaning goes beyond the literal meaning that could be discovered through grammatical analysis, (2) God, as the primary author of Scripture, included the spiritual meaning embedded in the text, and (3) the spiritual meaning may or may not have been understood by the human author. *Sensus plenior* gives more emphasis to the dual authorship of Scripture than does the historical-grammatical method. A very clear example comes from Paul's statement that the rock the Israelites drank from (Ex. 17:6; Num. 20:11) was actually Christ and that this rock followed them throughout their journey.

> They were all baptized into Moses in the cloud and in the sea. They all ate the same spiritual food and drank the same spiritual drink; for they drank from the spiritual rock that accompanied them, and that rock was Christ. 1 Cor. 10:2–4

This is certainly not the literal or historical meaning of the original text. Yet Paul does not use symbolic language that would indicate he is using it as a metaphor or allegorical language; he says, "That rock was Christ." Other examples include instances where the gospel writers applied an Old Testament text to an event in Jesus' life. William Klein uses Matthew 2:15 as an example. Matthew says that Jesus' return from Egypt was in fulfillment of Hosea 11:1. However, Klein states that Hosea's prophecy was related to an event fulfilled in his own time, and the natural reading could not be applied to Jesus.[120] Grant Osborne says that in Matthew's gospel alone there are ten passages in which Matthew states that some action related to Jesus was in fulfillment of an Old Testament prophecy.[121] The problem, according to Osborne, is that the original intent of the passage from a literal reading of the text does not reveal that the prophecy points to Christ. Evangelicals concede that Christ is the fulfillment of the Old Testament in general, but this argues against the idea that historical narratives should be read according to their literal, grammatical meaning. How did Matthew deduce that these passages were in reference to Christ? The only answer can be that the Holy Spirit revealed the spiritual meaning to Matthew. We can only conclude that at least some portions of the biblical text do have multiple layers of meaning.

Spirit and Scripture

The point that Brown has made and that evangelicals have not been able to refute is that when the New Testament writers quoted the Old Testament, they did not limit their interpretation to the literal, grammatical meaning of the words. Douglas Moo, Gordon Fee, and others acknowledge that Paul and other New Testament writers found spiritual meanings in the text that could not be discovered through its plain meaning, but they assert that although the apostles used this method of interpretation, modern readers are not enabled to discover such spiritual meanings—they seem to be implying that only apostles can discover the spiritual meaning of the text.[122]

The concern expressed by conservatives is that we have no cognitive tools for discovering or understanding the spiritual meaning of a text if it differs from the historical-grammatical meaning.[123] The Charismatic response is that we should not rely on human methods alone. The same Holy Spirit who enabled the first-century readers also enables us. God is the primary author of Scripture, and he is the source of the spiritual meanings embedded in the text. God actually calls us to participate in the unfolding of the biblical narratives as the Spirit brings forth new interpretations and applications for each new era of time.

Theological Narrative

The narrative approach to theology was commonplace in the early church and is now experiencing a retrieval. Narrative interpretation holds that God's message comes from the "story" rather than the details. We can see this in the parables of Jesus, in which some of the details are important to the story, and some are less important. For example, in the parable of the ten virgins, some interpreters want to assign a meaning to every detail, such as that the five foolish were told to go and purchase oil from the sellers. Overzealous interpreters will opine that the oil represents the Holy Spirit, and then they have to figure out who the sellers of the oil are. Such details are not important to the parable. The primary meaning of the parable is about being ready when the Lord returns; it is not about who has the Holy Spirit and who does not. Most parables have one primary meaning.

Narrative theology is less concerned with the historical background of the biblical narratives and focuses rather on the theological meaning of the text. Gary Comstock correctly claims that narrative theology is concerned with "religious claims embedded in stories."[124] A narrative can be oral or written, it connects parts of a story together into a whole, and it contains an overarching set of aims or values.[125] "More than half of the Old and New Testament is story."[126] The literal meaning of the story is based on the human author's intent, but it is axiomatic that the biblical writers were not just interested in recording the historical facts; they were retelling a story about God. In many cases, the historical facts were mere signs pointing to the deeper spiritual meaning.

The narrative approach to biblical interpretation is like a universal tool that can be used in many different ways. Postliberal theologians, especially from Yale Divinity School, popularized the narrative approach, but Pentecostals have widely used this approach with different presuppositions. Hans Frei is considered the father of postliberal narrative theology;[127] he and his colleagues are postliberal because while they do not necessarily deny the supernatural as do the liberals, they hold that the theological meaning of the biblical text is more important than the literal words. For postliberals such as Hans Frei, George Hunsinger, and George Lindbeck, theology is a science of the church—a science based on faith.[128] As a special type of science, as Karl Barth called it, theology does not have to correspond to any other type of science—it stands on its own merit. Each type of science has its own methods of practice and its own rules of verification and validation. Biblical interpretation is a science of the church, and therefore the church (God's people) are the experts on how the Bible should be interpreted. Frei and Carl Henry entered into a spirited debate over these issues because Henry wanted to ensure that Christian theology would remain rationally defensible.[129] Henry wants a theology that is rational and defensible in both the church and the academy. For Frei, theology is the property of the church; it is a science of the church and is validated by the church. It is ironic that postliberals have returned to the interpretative methods of the early church while moderates (and many conservatives) are still concerned with academic methods.

As with Brown and *sensus plenior* (described above), narrative is not limited to the grammatical meaning of the text. The church, prior to the Reformation, did not limit its hermeneutical methods to the historical-grammatical approach. Conservatives are concerned that the narrative approach is too subjective and could lead to all kinds of unfounded interpretations. This is why the Reformers (Luther, Calvin, Zwingli, etc.) insisted on a more literal approach to Scripture. If the narrative interpretation is not bound by literal and grammatical limitations, conservatives fear that it becomes subjective and may lead to the same abuses that the Reformers argued existed in the Catholic Church. The question that needs to be asked is this: How did God intend the Scriptures to be read and interpreted? The concern that we could be wrong in our interpretation is not the primary determinant because the historical-grammatical method may also lead to wrong conclusions.

Charismatic scholars have placed great emphasis on the community as the source of interpretative authority. Kenneth Archer, a Pentecostal scholar, holds that the spirit-filled community (*the church*) has the divine authority to read and interpret Scripture in fresh new ways that exceed the literal meaning of the text. In fact, Archer argues that the community is enabled to "produce" meaning from the biblical text.[130] Archer's model is commendatory in that he acknowledges that the Holy Spirit shapes the community and enables them to discern the spiritual meaning of the text. His model has at least two major weaknesses. First, as a classical Pentecostal, he insists that only Pentecostals have this ability. Archer does not recognize or acknowledge Spirit-filled individuals who do not identify as Pentecostal. The second weakness is his assertion that the community can create or produce meaning. This implies that they, in effect, create inspired meaning that is not embedded in the text by the Holy Spirit. The *sensus plenior* concept holds that the spiritual meaning must have been placed there by the Spirit; it is discovered by Spirit-filled humans, but it is not created or produced by humans, no matter how spiritual they may be. Mark Cartledge states that for Pentecostals, "The Holy Spirit inspires the contemporary reading of the text, just as he inspired the original authors."[131] We must understand this to mean that the text is inspired in a similar manner but not with the same degree of accuracy or infallibility.

Kevin Vanhoozer presents another approach to narrative theology.[132] Vanhoozer finds that we should learn principles from the biblical text and go on to apply those principles to everyday life. Vanhoozer likens theology to a four-act play in which the first three acts are scripted, and in the fourth act, the cast follows the trajectory of the first three acts but without a written script. The director (God) is still in control, but the participants speak and act according to what they learned in the previous acts.[133] This final act is where contemporary theology takes place; what is the director (God) saying to us, and what can we surmise, based on the script from the previous acts? Vanhoozer clearly identifies the Holy Spirit as remaining in control of the applicative process. The strength of Vanhoozer's proposal is that while we learn from the Scriptures, we apply those principles to real-life scenarios, and the application is canonical in the same sense that Scripture itself is canonical. To be canonical does not mean infallible, but it does mean it falls within God's intended domain for his communication with mankind. As with Archer's model, Vanhoozer agrees that the Holy Spirit shapes the individual to hear from God beyond the grammatical words of the text.

The narrative approach invites the reader to experience the biblical text as a present-day reality. Steven Land describes how narrative is applied by drawing the reader into the story.

Spirit and Scripture

> Pentecostals traveled in the Spirit forward or backward in time—back to Sinai, back to Calvary, back to Pentecost—forward to Armageddon, the Great White Throne Judgment, the Marriage Supper of the Lamb. Time and space were fused and transcended in the Spirit.[134]

Vanhoozer's model does the same; the reader participates in the biblical story and applies the principles to their own life. Certainly, the historian will object that God's words to Israel, "'For I know the plans I have for you,' declares the Lord, 'plans to prosper you and not to harm you, plans to give you hope and a future'" (Jer. 29:11), were given to Israel, and it is inappropriate to apply this to individuals today. The narrative approach will recognize that the original promise was to Israel, but that does not prohibit the modern reader from hearing God say the same thing to them. The question, of course, is whether the Spirit really speaks those words today or if our imaginations are just running amuck. Paul's use of allegory in Galatians may give us a clue. Paul tells us that "Abraham had two sons, one by the slave woman and the other by the free woman. ... These things are being taken figuratively: The women represent two covenants" (Gal. 4:21–26). Paul does not separate the literal meaning of the Old Testament story from the allegorical interpretation. The allegorical interpretation is true enough that Paul includes it in inspired Scripture. Hearing the voice of the Spirit always requires wisdom and discernment from the Spirit. This, however, should not preclude us from seeking God's will for us in every page of the text. One of the characteristics of the Charismatic church is that we believe God is working supernaturally in our time, and all God's people are invited to participate in what he is doing.

The Spirituality of the Interpreter

If we accept that the Bible is a spiritual book and has spiritual meanings that transcend the literal meaning, then we are faced with the question of how the reader should go about discovering and interpreting the spiritual meaning of the text. Conservatives are correct in their concerns that if everyone is free to adopt their own interpretation, it will lead to—in Vanhoozer's words—"interpretative anarchy."[135] This is the problem with reader-response theory, which holds that the meaning of a text is created not by the author, but in the mind of the reader. Each reader creates their own meaning to fit their own frame of reference. What we are proposing here is not reader response; rather, we are saying that reading and interpreting the Bible—hearing from God through the text—is the work of the Holy Spirit, and he enables Spirit-filled individuals to find meanings that often surpass the literal, grammatical meaning of the text.

There is strong biblical support for the fact that the Holy Spirit shapes the mind and spirit of the individual and enables us to hear his Spirit and understand spiritual truths. Paul makes use of the term *pneumatikoi*, which can mean spiritual ones or spiritual things. A spiritual person is one who has been transformed by the power of the Spirit. It does not refer to a specific experience that implies "You have arrived" and is accompanied by a specific demonstrative gift. Paul writes,

> The person without the Spirit does not accept the things that come from the Spirit of God but considers them foolishness and cannot understand them because they are discerned only through the Spirit. 1 Cor. 2:14

> The mind governed by the flesh is death, but the mind governed by the Spirit is life and peace. Rom. 8:6

The Charismatic person—the person filled with the Spirit and actively walking in the Spirit—is enabled to understand spiritual truths in a way that nonspiritual people are not. In the Parable of the Sower and the Soils, Jesus lamented that certain ones could not understand the word because their hearts were hard, and they had closed their eyes (Matt. 13). Spirituality is a quality of character that results from the active presence of the Holy Spirit in a person's life. It may refer to a permanent condition arrived at over time, such as "you who are spiritual" (Gal. 6:1), or it may refer to a more temporary condition, such as a heightened sense of spiritual awareness. John writes, "I was in the Spirit on the Lord's Day" (Rev. 1:10).

Not all Christians are spiritual. Paul writes to the Corinthians, "Brothers, I could not speak unto you as unto spiritual, but as unto carnal" (1 Cor 3:1). If these people were Christians, they had the Spirit (Rom. 8:9), and yet Paul says they were not spiritual people. Spirituality begins at salvation and grows over time as the individual yields to the leading of the Spirit. Some become spiritual very quickly, and some remain carnal. Paul could not speak to these carnal Christians as he wanted to because they would not be able to receive and understand his message.

The goal of spiritual transformation is a transformed mind. Spirituality affects our cognitive processes—the way we think, reason, and understand the world around us. Our spirituality is not disconnected from our minds; the two are fully integrated.

The mind governed by the flesh is death, but the mind governed by the Spirit is life and peace (Rom. 8:6); The mind governed by the flesh is hostile to God (Rom. 8:7); be transformed by the renewing of your mind" (Rom. 12:2); we have the mind of Christ (I Cor. 2:16); Let this mind be in you, which was also in Christ Jesus (Phil. 2:5); be made new in the attitude of your minds (Eph. 4:23); they are puffed up with idle notions by their unspiritual mind (Col. 2:18); they are men of depraved minds; (2 Tim. 3:8); be alert and of sober mind so that you may pray (1 Pet. 4:7).

James Beilby states, "Knowledge of God is participatory. In Scripture, knowledge of God is attained by those who choose to make themselves available to God for his purposes."[136] Spirituality is experiential and not just theoretical. It does not come about simply because we subscribe to the correct doctrine or have joined the right church. As demonstrated above, a person can be saved and not be spiritual (1 Cor. 3:1). Spiritual formation is initiated by God; we cooperate with God through grace, and God produces the internal change. Jesus states, "I am the true vine, and my Father is the gardener. He cuts off every branch in me that bears no fruit, while every branch that does bear fruit, he prunes so that it will be even more fruitful" **(Jn. 15:1–2)**. The Father nurtures us to secure our relationship with the vine and ensure the flow of all things spiritual from Christ the vine into the human branches.

Summary

Since this book is written specifically for Charismatics, we will summarize the chapter in a few short propositions that may be useful for the Charismatic reader.

One of the marks or characteristics of Charismatic people and churches is that we believe and expect God to continue speaking and revealing himself and his truths to us in fresh and exciting ways. We reject the view that the Bible is a sealed book and that the Spirit has nothing new to say.[137] What is revealed today does not challenge or contradict the written Scripture but finds additional meanings that are not apparent from the literal, grammatical words of the text. We read and interpret Scripture using the same methods as the New Testament writers while acknowledging that we do not have apostolic authority. The Bible is unique in its authority.

The Holy Spirit works through Spirit-filled individuals and groups in the interpretation of biblical texts and reveals truths that exceed historical and grammatical understanding. The prophetic nature of the Spirit combines spiritual knowledge and insights from various sources to develop a more complete understanding of God and his message to individuals and to the church. We do not read the Bible in a vacuum; our understanding of God is developed in the context of our full relationship with him. While the Bible is God's primary written word, it is not his only form of communicating with his people, and all God's methods of speaking into our lives should be received in concert with his word.

Chapter 7
Charismatic Spirituality

> I am again in the pains of childbirth until Christ is formed in you. Gal. 4:19

> You who are spiritual... Gal. 6:1

Christian spirituality refers to a condition in which the human mind, heart, and habits have been transformed by the Spirit of God to make the individual more like God. When Paul admonished the Galatians, "Brothers, if anyone is caught in any transgression, you who are spiritual should restore him" (Gal. 6:1 ESV), his statement assumes that some people are spiritual, and based on this spirituality, they are capable of making appropriate decisions on spiritual matters. On the other hand, Paul wrote to the Corinthians, saying, "Brothers, I could not speak unto you as unto spiritual, but as unto carnal" (1 Cor 3:1). So there were some Christians at Ephesus who were spiritual and some Christians at Corinth who were not. Some Christians are spiritual, and some are carnal. The word *carnal* or *fleshly* simply means to think in the natural way of the human mind, not the converted way of the Spirit. Can a Christian be carnal? Yes, of course. It simply means that their minds have not yet been transformed to think as Christ would think.[138] Not everyone who has the Spirit within the meaning of Romans 8:9 is

Charismatic Spirituality

spiritual. Paul is clear that every Christian has the Spirit, but not every Christian is spiritual.

Spiritual formation has become a topic of primary interest in recent decades. By titling this chapter Charismatic Spirituality, I am simply building a framework for approaching spirituality in continuity with Charismatic theology. While spiritual formation focuses on the process of being transformed, this chapter will focus primarily on the goal of transformation with secondary attention to methods of how to get there. Dallas Willard's book *The Spirit of the Disciplines* is the classic on how to achieve spiritual formation, and one of his later books, *Renovation of the Heart*, discusses the end goals of this transformation.[139] In this chapter, I want to discuss spirituality—both the process and the goals—through the lens of a Charismatic worldview. Spiritual formation refers to the work of the Holy Spirit in transforming the believer to become the person God desires them to be. It involves restoring the *imago Dei* (image of God) that was lost in the Adamic fall. We may know this as sanctification, but for some theologians, sanctification has come to mean our status in the sight of God as opposed to any real change in condition.[140] Spiritual formation is clearly focused on bringing change to the heart and mind of the believer. Spiritual formation aims to transform the human mind to think like Christ would have us think. Paul was very bold to declare that "we have the mind of Christ." Gaining the mind of Christ is the goal of spiritual formation, but to realize that goal requires full submission to the Spirit, and this state of mind does not come to its full maturity at the moment of salvation. Paul uses birth terminology to express his desire to see young Christians grow to maturity, a state in which "Christ is formed in you." Charismatics have a deep appreciation for the transformative work of the Spirit as demonstrated by a seeking after God (see Chapter 1).

Spiritual Awareness and Understanding

It has become fashionable to say, "I am spiritual but not religious." People who say this indicate that they have a spiritual awareness, but they are not affiliated with any organized religion.[141] They may be atheists, agnostics, or deists. Some are believers in Christ but not active participants in church. (They are believers but not disciples of Christ.) In contrast, biblical spirituality is always the result of the transformative work of the Holy Spirit. This transformative work is never a one-time experience, such as conversion; it is a relationship with the Spirit who continuously nurtures, corrects, and informs the spiritual person to become more spiritual. Spirituality requires a connection with the vine from which the person draws nourishment and is pruned by the gardener to cut off unhealthy elements and increase spirituality (Jn. 15:1–8).

The new birth is the beginning of the spiritual journey, but one experience does not make a person truly spiritual. The human spirit can become trained by the Holy Spirit so that it is connected to and aware of the Holy Spirit's presence. The non-Christian who says, "I am spiritual but not religious," attributes their spiritual awareness to human ability. Karl Rahner, by contrast, argues that all humans are created in the image of God, and we are "spiritual" as part of God's design. In Rahner's words, we are "transcendent" in the same way, but not to the same degree, that God is transcendent.[142] The question that must be asked is to what degree did humankind retain this transcendence or spirituality after the Adamic fall? Some would argue that we lost all aspects of spirituality in the fall, but Rahner is saying that transcendence is part of human nature. He does not mean human nature as an element separate from God but human nature as an element of God's design. In Rahner's view, a non-Christian can be spiritual, and such spirituality would be enhanced through salvation. The point we want to observe from Rahner is that God designed us to be able to communicate with him. When God speaks, the human spirit has a God-given ability to hear and understand. That ability to hear

Charismatic Spirituality

and observe spiritual things was damaged in the fall but not destroyed. Christian spirituality, and more specifically, Charismatic spirituality, is restored through the continuous presence of the Holy Spirit. Paul is confident that the spiritual people in Galatia could restore the fallen brother or sister because they are able to understand the will of the Spirit concerning the fallen person (Gal. 6:1).

A person who is spiritually aware is always on the alert to observe and listen to what the Spirit may be doing and saying. So when the apostles and prophets gathered for prayer, they were able to hear the Spirit say, "Set apart for me, Barnabas and Saul." Recognizing that there were prophets in the group and most apostles also prophesied from time to time, it is still not clear how the Spirit spoke to them or how they received this revelation.

> Now in the church at Antioch, there were prophets and teachers: Barnabas, Simeon called Niger, Lucius of Cyrene, Manaen (who had been brought up with Herod the Tetrarch), and Saul. While they were worshiping the Lord and fasting, the Holy Spirit said, "Set apart for me Barnabas and Saul for the work to which I have called them." So after they had fasted and prayed, they placed their hands on them and sent them off. Acts 13:1–3

What we should understand is that walking in the Spirit—having spiritual awareness—gives a person a greater ability to sense and understand what God is doing and saying. When Paul was preaching in Lystra, "There sat a man who was lame. He had been that way from birth and had never walked. He listened to Paul as he was speaking. Paul looked directly at him, saw that he had faith to be healed" (Acts 13:8–9), how is it that Paul saw that this man had faith to be healed? Was this the spiritual gift of a word of knowledge? Nearly all supernatural gifts require an understanding of what God's will is in that particular situation. There needs to be an understanding of what may be blocking healing from taking place, insight into whether there is demonic activity, and other such insights.

Spiritual gifts do not operate in a vacuum. They operate as the Holy Spirit desires to manifest his work, primarily in the body of Christ, but also in the world. Sometimes the will of the Spirit may be revealed at the moment of the need, but also, the knowledge and wisdom may be instilled in the believer as they grow in spiritual maturity. A prophet's understanding of the total revelation of God is built layer upon layer; that is to say, prophecy is progressive as it builds on the revelation previously given. Daniel studied the prophecies of Jeremiah to understand how long Israel would remain in captivity, and Daniel added additional prophetic understanding to what he learned from studying Jeremiah (Dan. 9:2). Likewise, the New Testament apostles studied the Old Testament, but they also added prophetic insight to better understand what God was saying to them. Spiritual understanding of what the Spirit has done and said before is helpful in laying a foundation for what He is revealing to us today. In Chapter 6 of this book, we discussed the dynamic relationship between Spirit and Word. A person cannot interpret the spiritual meaning of the biblical text unless the reader is living in the Spirit. In the same manner, a person cannot interpret the Spirit's work in the present time without a large measure of spiritual awareness and understanding.

God speaks and reveals himself and his will, not only through words but also through his actions. Modern-day "prophets" have spoken out on everything from earthquakes to elections, but their accuracy rate is very questionable. Spirituality is not a one-time gift that qualifies a person to be a spokesperson for God. Spirituality is a relationship that builds and progresses over time. Living in the Spirit allows God to manifest himself through you with gifts of his choice. Being aware of the Spirit's presence allows you to hear his voice and see his hand at work.

The Mind of Christ

> Do not conform to the pattern of this world but be transformed by the renewing of your mind. Rom. 12:2

> We have the mind of Christ.... 1 Cor. 2:16

The human mind is at the control center of our being. All of our thoughts, desires, and actions come through the mind. Paul warned us not to be "conformed to the world" (Rom. 12:2). J. B. Phillips' translation has it, "Don't let the world around you squeeze you into its own mold." The pressures of everyday life mold the mind in ways we are not aware of. The thoughts and words that go into the mind have the potential to take root and affect the way we think and the way we see the world. The mind is the gateway to the human spirit. In a previous chapter, we discussed the union of the Holy Spirit and the human spirit. A spiritual person, as described in this chapter, is one in whom the human spirit is in unity with the divine Spirit. Dallas Willard writes,

> You have a spirit within you, and it has been formed. It has taken on a specific character. I have a spirit and it has been formed. This is true of everyone. The human spirit is an inescapable, fundamental aspect of every human being, and it takes on whatever character it has from the experiences and the choices that we have lived through or made in our past.[143]

Willard also asserts that divine revelation—that which God reveals to us—comes "mainly in the form of thought."[144] That is to say, what God reveals, whether through Scripture, experience, observation, or that still, small voice within, enters our being as thoughts. Before we can assimilate those thoughts, they are screened through the filter of our previously established thoughts, including our worldview. All new thoughts are weighed against our presuppositions, and the new thoughts are reviewed, evaluated, and adjusted prior to acceptance or rejection. The spiritual person is someone whose mind has been renewed by the Holy Spirit to think with the mind of Christ. In its full stage of maturity, new thoughts and observations will be evaluated against this new mind that is in conformity with the mind of Christ. In Paul's letter to the Romans, he chastised the ungodly because "they did not think it worthwhile to retain the knowledge of God, so God gave them over to a depraved mind" (Rom. 1:28). Paul implies that even prior to salvation, they had the ability to retain a knowledge of God—as much as can be learned through natural observation—but they chose not to do so.

The transformed mind is not an empty mind; it is creative. I will admit that I was appalled when I first read someone referring to the imagination as an instrument of God. I previously thought of the imagination as either an evil place ("And God saw that the wickedness of man was great in the earth, and that every imagination of the thoughts of his heart was only evil continually" (Gen. 6:5 KJV) or a place of fiction. I had to have a change of view to see that imagination is a gift from God. The imagination has been corrupted by the Adamic fall and further by the corruption of the mind that comes through our continued disobedience. Along with a transformed mind, we have available to us a transformed imagination, and that imagination can be a creative insight into the mind of Christ. A Spirit-directed imagination is not a source of evil and fiction but an instrument of the Holy Spirit. The "born again" mind has been reclaimed, and the image of God is at least partially restored. The mind "governed by the Spirit" (Rom. 8:6) may receive an impulse from a thought, an image, a word, or a sound that becomes a symbol on the scratch pad. One symbol connects to another symbol, and eventually, the dots are connected to form a new image—and the journey begins. The mind of the flesh will travel down very dark and destructive roads, but the mind under the influence of the Spirit will be drawn to God.

The sanctified imagination can be creative and trustworthy. The early church fathers used Spirit-directed imagination in the interpretation of Scripture. Conservatives today, under the influence of Enlightenment philosophy, rely on human reasoning as the best way to interpret Scripture. The early theologians from Origen to Augustine relied on the Spirit to reveal analogy and allegory within Scripture. Jesus used an analogy in his "the kingdom is like . . ." parables. D. A. Carson writes concerning the different genres of Scripture:

> Each genre has a slightly different way of appealing to us, of making its impact on us. Together they do even more than instruct our minds: they fire our imaginations, prompt us to meditate, call up mental pictures, invite us to memorize, appeal to our emotions, shame us when our thoughts or actions are tawdry and unworthy, and make our spirits leap for joy.[145]

Symbols have a communicative power in the imagination that exceeds words; symbols can expand in creative ways. Paul Ricoeur refers to it as the "productive imagination" and finds that it can bridge the unknown to the known.[146] The human imagination is only an evil place when left at the disposal of an evil mind, but under the direction of the Holy Spirit, the imagination can transcend the boundaries of the human mind and receive what God is saying in ways that cannot be discovered through logic or science. The transformed mind is not a blank slate or an empty place; it is full of the word and wonders of God.

Spirituality and Holiness

The definition of holiness is debated as much as the meaning of Baptism in the Spirit. In this book, we define holiness as that condition in which a person loves God with all the heart and with all the soul and with all the mind and loves their neighbor as themself (Matt. 22:37–39). Jesus went on to say, "All the Law and the Prophets hang on these two commandments." Holiness is the result of the Spirit's work transforming the mind to think like Christ, the heart to desire the things of Christ, and the habits to live as Christ.

Many Reformed theologians hold that holiness, also known as sanctification, is entirely the work of the Spirit and requires no active participation on the part of the Christian.[147] According to this view, the righteousness of Christ is imputed or bestowed upon the believer. Just as the believer is elect (predestined) to salvation through justification, that same work of the Spirit brings sanctification. The issue here is whether sanctification merely means "set apart to God" or if it also includes a change in the heart and mind of the believer. Classical Reformed theology, following Calvin, holds that justification and sanctification are based on the imputed work of Christ and represent a change in status but not a change in the condition of the believer. I refer to this as the classical Reformed position because some Reformed theologians hold that humans do have some responsibility to cooperate in the process and pursuit of holiness.[148] J. I. Packer is among the Reformed theologians who understand that holiness requires a change of condition as well as a change of status. Packer writes, "Holiness has to do with my heart. A holy person's motivating aim, passion, desire, longing, aspiration, goal, and drive is to please God."[149]

Luther complicated the matter by equating sanctification with righteousness. He then argued for "primary sanctification," which comes with regeneration, and then "secondary sanctification," which requires our cooperation.[150] The Reformers focused most of their doctrinal development on primary sanctification with much less emphasis on how that should be lived out. Sanctification normally refers to something that is set apart or dedicated to God. Holiness can mean the same thing, except when it is stated as an imperative: "Be holy, because I am holy" (1 Pet. 1:16).[151] Holiness is a cooperative effort, just like the command to "be filled with the Spirit" (Eph. 5:18). There can be no doubt that to be filled with the Spirit is the result of God's work within us. However, Paul's admonishment is necessary because we are called to seek after God. "But seek first his kingdom and his righteousness, and all these things will be given to you as well" (Matt. 6:33). Holiness, like being filled with the Spirit, is God's work, but it comes to those who seek after him. J. I. Packer writes, "Prayer and holiness are learned in a similar way as commitments are made, habits are formed, and battles are fought."[152] Holiness is an internal condition that is reflected in outward behavior. In the Old Testament, holiness was mostly observed through outward obedience to the Laws of Moses. It was a daily reminder to the people of their obligation to serve God and place hm first. Second, it was part of their identity as the people of God. Circumcision, sabbath keeping, and refraining from idol worship were unique to Israel and marked them as God's people. Anyone who refused to keep these laws was to be cut off from the people of Israel. Not only did this protect the Israelites and bind them together in unity, but it also bore witness to the other nations that they worshiped a unique God. While New Testament holiness is less dependent on written laws, it nevertheless has some of the same purposes and characteristics. Sanctification of the heart changes us so that we love God and love our neighbors. This inward condition is meaningless if it does not result in outward action and lifestyle. Paul described love in these terms:

> Love is patient, love is kind. It does not envy, it does
> not boast, it is not proud. It does not dishonor others,
> it is not self-seeking, it is not easily angered, it keeps
> no record of wrongs. Love does not delight in evil but
> rejoices with the truth. It always protects, always
> trusts, always hopes, always perseveres. 1 Cor. 13:4–7

Love that only exists in the heart but is not displayed outwardly is not true love. Holiness that exists only inwardly is not true holiness. That is why Scripture can demand that we "be holy"—it is something we are and also something we do. Inward holiness is a condition of the heart and only comes about through the transformative power of God. It is summed up in the two great commands: love God and love your neighbor (Matt. 22:37–39). This type of holiness is not automatic or immediate upon salvation. It requires a continuous seeking after and submission to God. It requires that we reject our fleshly desires and choose daily the ways of God. Holiness is inseparable from spirituality (see Chapter 7). If God is at work in one's life, he will produce holiness. The only question is a matter of timing. If we seek after God and surrender to the urging of his Spirit, holiness comes more quickly than if we give in to our own selfish desires.

Historically, Pentecostals and Charismatics have wrestled with the connection between holiness and spiritual power. An early split developed in the Pentecostal movement over the issue of when holiness begins. Many of the early Pentecostals taught sanctification as a definite second work of the Spirit following salvation. This resulted in a soteriology that included three works of grace: salvation, sanctification, and Baptism in the Spirit. Each of these was believed to be a distinct and knowable event to be experienced by the believer. It was believed that a person could not receive Baptism with the Spirit unless they had first been sanctified. Pentecostal theology was developed from Wesleyan-Arminian theology with regard to sanctification and holiness. William Durham, beginning in about 1910, made an impact on Pentecostal theology by preaching "the finished work of Calvary"—meaning that sanctification is included in justification at the moment of salvation. Similar to the Reformed view, the "finished work view" holds that sanctification means set apart, not changed. A person is set apart by Christ and declared righteous at the moment of salvation. The Assemblies of God were formed about the time of the finished work controversy, and they took a middle position.[153] They agreed with Durham that sanctification as a separate work of grace was not necessary to prepare one for Baptism in the Spirit. Thus, the three works of grace were reduced to two: Salvation and Baptism in the Spirit.[154] However, the Assemblies retained the Wesleyan emphasis that holiness requires cooperation and pursuit by the believer. Holiness is a change in condition and not simply the imputed righteousness of Christ. Wesleyan-Armenian theology holds that while sanctification is a progressive work, it is normative for the believer to reach a point of "entire sanctification," which Wesley described as perfect love.[155] Critics often assert that Wesleyans believe in "sinless perfection," but that is not the case. For Wesley and his followers, entire sanctification means a state in which the person does not willfully commit any sin. Wesley acknowledged that a sanctified person may still commit sins of ignorance and unintentional offenses—but the person would have a pure heart toward God and people. For Wesleyans, sanctification begins with progressive growth in grace but also includes a point in time (a crisis moment) when entire sanctification occurs.

Having discussed the range of views on holiness, we return to the main thesis of this chapter. A spiritual person is one who has been transformed by the Spirit and continues to live under the Spirit's influence (Rom. 8:6). Holiness cannot be viewed as a static condition based on the imputed work of Christ or on a work of the Spirit that happened at salvation unless it includes an ongoing work of the Spirit that produces an actual change in the life of the believer. As we have defined it, holiness is a condition in which a person loves God with all the heart and with all the soul and with all the mind and loves their neighbor as themself. Holiness is the result of the Spirit's work transforming the mind to think like Christ, the heart to desire the things of Christ, and the habits to live as Christ.

We cannot claim that the Charismatic view of holiness is somehow superior to other views or even that it is unique. Our purpose here is to issue a reminder of our responsibility as the Spirit-filled people of God. Holiness requires not just cooperation but the active pursuit of the heart of God. It requires submission to the Spirit, giving priority to God's will over our own will. It means denying the call of our own flesh and yielding to the call of the Spirit as he speaks through Scripture and through his "still small voice" within. As Charismatics, we are people of the Spirit. We cannot read the Bible as a legal text (see Chapter 6), but we must learn to hear the voice of the Spirit as he speaks to us in a personal way. Evangelist G. D. Watson

(1845–1924) penned this reminder about the personalization of God's sanctifying work in our loves.

> If God has called you to be really like Jesus, He will draw you into a life of crucifixion and humility, and put upon you such demands of obedience, that you will not be able to measure yourself by other Christians; and in many ways, He will seem to let other good people do things which He will never let you do.
>
> Other Christians and ministers, who seem very religious and useful, can push themselves, pull wires, and work schemes to carry out their Christian goals, but these things you simply cannot do. Others may boast of their work or their writings or their success, but the Holy Spirit will not allow you to do any such thing, and if you ever try it, He will lead you into some deep mortification that will make you despise yourself and all your good works.
>
> The Holy Spirit will rebuke you for little words or deeds or even feelings or for wasting your time, which other Christians never seem to be concerned about, but you must make up your mind that God is an infinite Sovereign, and He has a right to do whatever He pleases with His own. He may not explain to you a thousand things which puzzle your reason in the way He deals with you, but if you will just submit yourself to Him in all things, He will wrap you up in a jealous love and bestow upon you many blessing which come only to those who are very near to His heart.[156]

Watson's words serve as a reminder that our holiness and our obedience are not measured by the performance of other people. God may allow others to live in concert with the moral values of the culture, but we are called to a higher standard. Rather than seeking legal loopholes that would allow us to live like the world, we should ask God to empower us to live as Christ. We should consider it a blessing when God chastises us and calls us to a higher standard because when he does, he will also empower us to live to a higher standard. David DeSilva refers to Paul's use of "the indicative and the imperative" mood in Galatians 6:25.[157] The Greek indicative is a statement of fact: *since we live by the Spirit*. The Greek imperative is a command: since you live by the Spirit, *let us also keep in step with the Spirit*. Holiness is frequently stated as an imperative. Jesus said, "Be perfect, therefore, as your heavenly Father is perfect (Matt. 5:48), and Peter carried an Old Testament command forward to the New Testament, saying, "Be holy for I am holy" (1 Pet. 1:15–16). An imperative implies we have both the duty and the ability to comply. The biblical definition of *perfect* means to be all that God intends for you to be. God has not set impossible standards, but with the standard, he grants the power to meet it.

Walking in Power

Along with everything else discussed above, spirituality results in power. Spirituality is the continuous work of the Holy Spirit in the human spirit, and this continuous flow and work of the Spirit produces the fruit of the Spirit. By fruit, I mean all the products of the Spirit—not just the nine fruits mentioned in Galatians 5. The Spirit produces holiness, thoughtfulness, kindness, love, and power. Power is one aspect of spirituality. Power is not limited to the working of miracles, but it includes all of the work the Holy Spirit does through your life and mine. Donald Gee, one of the early leaders in the Assemblies of God, lamented that too many Pentecostals overemphasize the gift of tongues to the neglect of other gifts, such as preaching and teaching. For Gee, preaching is also a display of power.[158]

Power is exercised when several factors come into confluence: the actual presence of the Holy Spirit, an awareness of God's plan and the desire to take action, and faith-based boldness for the Christian to step out and take action. The spiritual person (the person walking in unity with the Spirit) is an instrument of the Spirit. Such a person is more likely to be aware of their spiritual gifts, more likely to be developing and growing in their gifts, more likely to have the boldness to act, and more likely to hear the voice of the Spirit as he directs the believer in ministry.

The spiritual person does not hear the Spirit speaking continuously to them like an earbud. Too often, we meet people who claim that God speaks to them throughout the day, even on the most minute details. The apostle Paul is an example of a person walking in the Spirit, but he did not always know God's will at every moment of his journey. In Acts 16, we read that Paul and his group desired to go to Phrygia and Galatia, but the Holy Spirit would not allow them to go there (Acts 16:6). Then they tried to go to Bithynia, but again the Spirit would not permit them to go there (Acts 16:7). After both these doors were closed, Paul saw a vision of a man from Macedonia saying, "Come over into Macedonia, and help us" (Acts 16:9). Paul's attempts to go to Phrygia, Galatia, and Bithynia indicate that he did not know God's will until those doors were closed, but he was sensitive enough to the Spirit that he recognized it was the Spirit closing the door. He was also spiritual enough that he could receive the vision of the man from Macedonia. It would be rare for a nonspiritual person to have such a vision. Walking in power requires not only access to the Spirit's power but also access to the Spirit's wisdom. Before one attempts to move mountains, one must know if God wants the mountains to be moved.

To walk in power also refers to our relationship with others. Jesus' reference to "power" in Luke 24:49 and repeated in Acts 1:8 was in reference to bearing witness to the gospel. The spiritual person is empowered to speak into the lives of other people. As the Holy Spirit speaks to the human spirit, so also one human spirit can speak nonverbally to another human spirit. (See Chapter 2.) The spiritual person is an instrument of the Holy Spirit—"rivers of living water will flow from within them" (Jn. 7:38). This flowing of the Spirit out from the spiritual person flows to other people, bringing them into the presence of God. The laying on of hands is more than symbolic; it is in fulfillment of Jesus' prophetic words about the flowing of the Spirit from one person and touching others.

Summary

The word *spiritual* is now being used in many different contexts. A search of journal articles and blog posts will discover references to *spiritual* and *spirituality* in everything from health care and counseling to leadership journals. Many of the sources have no apparent connection with anything religious and point to the popular adage "I am spiritual but not religious."[159] We should not throw out the term because it is misused by non-Christians. In Christianity, the term *spiritual* must have the same meaning that Paul gives it in references such as Galatians 4:19 and 6:1 and 1 Corinthians 3:1. A spiritual person is one in whom the human mind, heart, and habits have been transformed by the Spirit of God to make the individual more like God. One does not become spiritual by a single completed act. To be spiritual means that the Holy Spirit dwells permanently and actively in and through the person. This continuous flow of the Spirit produces an awareness of His presence; a mind that thinks like Christ; and holiness of thoughts, desires, and actions, as well as the powerful works of the Spirit.

Chapter 8
Participation with Christ

Charismatic Christians not only expect God to do great and supernatural wonders in our time and in our midst but also to participate with him in his work. Jesus chose twelve from among his disciples and appointed them as apostles—to whom he gave power and authority—to assist him in his work (Matt. 10:1; Mk. 6:7; Lk. 9:1). In this chapter, we are interested in finding the normative call for New Testament Christians.

Participation in the Old Testament

In the Old Testament, the call to participate was limited to a few people, mostly kings, prophets, and priests. The Holy Spirit did not live within individuals except those who were anointed for a specific ministry. John says that prior to Pentecost as "the Spirit had not been given" (Jn. 7:39). He means that while the Spirit was given to certain specific individuals, he (the Spirit) was not given to every believer. The Levites were called to serve in the Tabernacle, and the sons of Aaron were called to minister before the Lord as priests, and they alone were allowed to offer sacrifices at the alter (Num. 8:1–29, 18:1–7). Anyone other than a son of Aaron who attempted to minister at the alter was to be put to death (Num. 18:6–7).

The first kings of Israel—Saul, David, and Solomon—were called and anointed by God, and God specifically placed his Spirit within them (1 Sam. 10:1–9, 16:13; 1 Kgs. 3:10–14). David was a type of

Christ, and the Messiah was a "son of David" (Matt. 1:1, 9:27, 20:30). Promises made to David were ultimately fulfilled through Christ as the Messiah (Lk. 1:32). The kings were chosen by God based on his own sovereign will, and they had no other qualifications and did not need to come through any particular tribe or family. The same is true of the judges: Othniel, Ehud, Deborah, Gideon, Jephthah, and Samson. Moses was a unique prophet-judge-ruler. When Miriam and Aaron challenged Moses' leadership, God said:

> When there is a prophet among you, I, the Lord, reveal myself to them in visions, I speak to them in dreams. But this is not true of my servant Moses; he is faithful in all my house. With him, I speak face to face, clearly and not in riddles; he sees the form of the Lord. Why then were you not afraid to speak against my servant Moses? Num. 12:6–8

The conclusion is that the call to ministry in the Old Testament was unique and personal, and no one dared to join a ministry rank (priest, son of Aaron, prophet, or judge) unless God called and anointed them.

Participation in the New Testament

Joel prophesied and Peter repeated on the Day of Pentecost,

> In the last days, God says, I will pour out my Spirit on all people. Your sons and daughters will prophesy, your young men will see visions, your old men will dream dreams. Even on my servants, both men and women, I will pour out my Spirit in those days, and they will prophesy. Acts 2:17–18

The text does not actually say that everyone will prophesy, dream dreams, and have visions, but it does say that "all people" will have the Spirit. This represents a dramatic change from the situation in the Old Testament, in which the Spirit was only given to a select few who were chosen for ministry. John's statement that the Spirit was not yet given has now come to an end; the Spirit is now given to all who receive Christ through saving faith. The Spirit is now available to everyone, and everyone is invited to participate in the ministry work of God.

There are three attributes to the call to ministry in the New Testament: (1) power, (2) placement in the body, and (3) submission to authority.

The first attribute is power. Jesus told his disciples to remain in Jerusalem until they had been filled with the Holy Spirit with the evidence of power (Acts 1:8). This command was given to the eleven apostles who had already been commissioned and sent forth to preach, heal, and cast out demons. However, after Jesus departed the earth, they needed an anointing of power that would stand even in the absence of Jesus' physical body. Participation in the New Testament is totally dependent on the power of the Spirit. We have said elsewhere in this book (Chapters 2 and 3) that spiritual gifts are the norm for a New Testament church. The Bible does not provide any other model for how a New Testament church is to operate.

The second attribute is placement in the body. God placed everyone with spiritual gifts into the body of Christ—the church—in the exact position in the body where he wants each person to function (1 Cor. 12:12–27). This goes beyond specifying what gift(s) you are to receive; it also includes how you are to function in relationship to other members of the body. No Christian is called to operate in the spiritual gifts on their own, isolated and independent of the body of Christ—the church. Paul uses physical body parts as metaphors for the members of the spiritual body. Just as a physical body has eyes, ears, feet, and hands, so a spiritual body has members that work together to meet the needs of the total group and of the individuals in the group. The ear is useless if it is disconnected from the body, and in fact, it will soon atrophy and die. In the mid–twentieth century, there were many independent "healing ministries" that toured America and Europe. They were often independent of any denomination, association, or accountability, and many of them fell into moral failure. There are no biblical examples of independent ministers—be they healing ministers or prophets—operating outside the church. At the very least, a nondenominational or independent ministry should have an accountability board and should work cooperatively with other churches and ministries. Billy Graham would not hold a crusade unless a plurality of pastors in the city agreed to support the crusade. Our call to participate in the work of God is a call to participate in the work of the church as members of the church.

The third attribute is submission to authority. The call to participate in the work of the church necessarily requires that we submit to the authorities God has placed over us. This becomes complicated and challenging in the modern church, where the majority of growth is occurring in nondenominational churches. Authority and discipline are nearly absent from most evangelical churches. However, the invitation and empowerment to participate in God's work is never an invitation to operate independently.

The New Testament brought a total change in how people participate in the work of God. Rather than just a few people with the Spirit, as was the case in the Old Testament, the New Covenant sees the coming of the Holy Spirit upon all people. In the Old Testament temple, only the priest could enter the Holy Place to worship and offer sacrifices. Only the High Priest could enter the Most Holy Place (the Holy of Holies), and that only once per year. The Holiest of Holies was separated from the rest of the temple by a curtain. When Jesus died, the curtain was torn, signifying that the way into God's presence was now open to his people (Matt. 27:51; Mk. 15:38; Lk. 23:45; Heb. 10:20).

Ministry in Context

Paul was very concerned with maintaining unity and peace within the church. He advised slaves that if they could gain their freedom, they should do so, but if not, they should be content to remain as slaves (1 Cor. 7:21). Women should maintain a proper head covering because to do otherwise might set a bad example for the angels (1 Cor. 11:10). People should not speak in tongues in a public assembly without interpretation because an uninformed person might think they are strange (1 Cor. 14:23). Paul's obsession with unity and orderliness—goals he almost never achieved in the churches under his leadership—had to be placed in the context of the religious and social mores of his day. He worried that people would think a woman with short hair might be a prostitute because "it is a disgrace for a woman to have her hair cut off" (1 Cor. 11:6). Paul advised the people in Galatia not to become circumcised (Gal. 5:2), but he had Timothy circumcised to please the Jewish believers in Jerusalem (Acts 16:3). Paul's desire to maintain unity meant that the opinions and values of other people—inside and outside the church—were valuable norms to be maintained. Slaves and women should stay in the positions assigned to them by society if breaking out would cause disharmony. There was no thought in Paul's mind that the church should take a leading role in social transformation. Paul is able to draw a dichotomy between our status as saved individuals in Christ and our status in public positions. "There is neither Jew nor Gentile, neither slave nor free, nor is there male and female, for you are all one in Christ Jesus" (Gal. 3:28). Neither slave nor free, male nor female only pertains to our salvation in Christ—not our position in the church. Paul was not able to see beyond his immediate social context. Preserving unity was more important than individual liberties.

The difficult challenge for believers today is how we are to do as Paul did—respect the social mores of the day while remaining true to God. If the social context in which Paul wanted to maintain unity changes over time, how do we continue to maintain unity in ever-changing contexts? The predominate method among evangelicals has been to ignore social context and retain fidelity to the context of the first century. However, this approach may achieve the opposite result of that which is desired. Slaves should not be content to remain in slavery; breaking out will not cause disharmony in the church or in society. Women with short hair should not worry that they will be considered prostitutes or that the angels will misunderstand.

There is not time or space for a full-scale discussion of the role of women (or slaves) in ministry except to say that God's plan for the New Testament is all-inclusive participation in ministry. Anything short of that would have to be based on solid exegesis of theological truth. Many of the issues discussed by Paul were based on situations related to first-century society and the desire to maintain peace and unity between the church and society and between Jews and Gentiles. Every person who is born again and filled with the Spirit is invited to participate in the work of God. We are empowered by the Spirit specifically to do the work of the kingdom. The types of work and specific assignments are determined by the guidance of the Spirit and the gifts granted.

Summary

The gifts of the Spirit are given to each believer according to the sovereign will of God, and the believer is placed into the body of Christ according to God's plan for the church. The coming of the Spirit in the New Testament opened a new epoch in which spiritual gifts are offered to every believer. The purpose of the gifts is for us to participate in God's work within the framework of the church. Christ continues his missional work upon the earth, and we are invited to participate in that work. Some people are called to full-time paid positions, but everyone is called and invited to participate in some way. The context in which ministry takes place is important, and the context is ever changing. The church is tempted by two mistakes. The first mistake is to ignore context and insist everyone who wants to come to Christ should adopt our customs, vocabulary, and habits regardless of the theological value. The opposite mistake is to allow society to determine the values of the church. Jesus left his disciples behind to be "in the world but not of the world" (Jn. 17:15–21). We are in the world for a purpose; we are a people on mission. To effectively accomplish that mission, we must interact with the world while resisting the temptation to become like the world in spirit and beliefs.

Participation with Christ means that we are united with him, which is symbolized in baptism and communion. In this state of participation, we are carried along by the Spirit and united with Christ—our spirit with his Spirit—participating with him in the work that he continues to do through the Holy Spirit. Jesus tells us that we not only participate with him, but we are also fully integrated with the Trinity. "On that day you will realize that I am in my Father, and you are in me, and I am in you" (Jn. 14:20). We can participate in Christ's work because his Spirit is in us, and we are in Him. The awareness of God's presence is a chief characteristic of the Charismatic life.

Chapter 9
The Role of the Charismatic Church

The Charismatic church is not separate from other Christian churches; Jesus only has one church. However, within that great church, there are various bodies of believers joined together by grace but differing in culture, emphasis, and missional context. The churches mentioned in the New Testament were similar in some respects but very different in others. Peter described what we have in common in these words: "Those who have been chosen according to the foreknowledge of God the Father, through the sanctifying work of the Spirit, to be obedient to Jesus Christ and sprinkled with his blood" (1 Pet. 1:2). Within this great group, some emphasize the Charismatic life more than others. We assert that churches with a Charismatic emphasis have unique opportunities to participate with the Holy Spirit in his missional work and to personally experience the Spirit's gifts of grace and power.

This chapter will discuss charismatic theology from the perspective of the church. Spiritual gifts and individuals with gifts do not operate in isolation from the church—the body of Christ. In this chapter, we will discuss the role of the church in five primary areas: spiritual formation, prayer, stewardship of spiritual gifts, holiness, and healing. One of the primary responsibilities of Christ's ministers is to equip and build up the members of the body for works of service. This is true in all churches, not just Charismatic ones, but Charismatics are uniquely equipped and uniquely challenged in the areas of spiritual giftedness.

The Role of the Church in Spiritual Formation

> So Christ himself gave the apostles, the prophets, the evangelists, the pastors and teachers, to equip his people for works of service, so that the body of Christ may be built up. Eph. 4:11–12

> Now you are the body of Christ, and each one of you is a part of it. And God has placed in the church first of all apostles, second prophets, third teachers, then miracles, then gifts of healing, of helping, of guidance, and of different kinds of tongues. 1 Cor. 12:27–28

We discussed spirituality in Chapter 7. Here, I want to discuss the role of the church in promoting spiritual formation. Spiritual formation must come before spiritual gifts. Many churches have a narrow focus concerning their areas of responsibility. For some churches, that focus is community service or social justice; for some, it is evangelism; and for some, it is Bible knowledge. Regardless of what the church believes to be its primary mission, the people will not be equipped to fulfill the mission and remain healthy themselves if they are not fed a healthy diet and nurtured in their development. A healthy spiritual diet must be well balanced and include nourishment to encourage, motivate, and heal the person in addition to equipping them on how to do the mission of the church. If the church focuses on evangelism and the people go out sharing their faith door to door, but they are empty inside, they will soon experience fatigue and burnout. There are many churches that focus on community service—such as care for the poor or social justice—and they are able to attract many people, including non-Christians, to their cause. But some people are simply working

The Role of the Charismatic Church

from a humanitarian basis rather than from a spiritual connection with Christ. Barna Research Reports:

> Recent data show that Americans are trending toward spiritual openness. As of October 2022, Barna data show three out of four U.S. adults (74%) say they want to grow spiritually. Additionally, the same proportion (77%) say they believe in a higher power.[160]

The Charismatic church is uniquely qualified to help the 74 percent who want to grow spiritually. Many of them are not Christians and may very well fit in that "spiritual but not religious" category. However, their interest in spirituality is a starting point for evangelistic conversation. A Charismatic church, by definition, is one that operates under the power of the Spirit and emphasizes that aspect in its normal functions. Spiritual formation comes through teaching, preaching, and discipling of the people: in other words, *shepherding*. The shepherd knows the needs of each individual person and tailors the nourishment and care to their needs. To disciple a person does not just mean that you have a buffet of religious education programs; it is more personal than that. Most large churches have handed the pastor/shepherding responsibilities off to small groups, which go by a variety of different names. Small groups are wonderful, but most of the small group leaders have no training in how to be shepherds. If the church is too large for the pastoral staff to shepherd, and the small group leaders do not have the training or the giftings, it seems apparent that very little shepherding will get accomplished.

The role of the church in promoting spiritual growth in the members is to provide the group processes whereby the need for spiritual growth is emphasized, and the spiritual disciplines are modeled. Through the preaching, the teaching, and the example set by the leadership team, members of the congregation need to recognize their own areas of weakness and realize that God has a more victorious and powerful life available to them. Some people have struggled for so long against their own weakness that they accept the struggle as a way of life, and they become spiritually and emotionally frustrated. They do not experience God's power in their life; instead, their lives are characterized by guilt and defeat. They truly need a spiritual transformation, but they do not know how or where to start. There is strong evidence to suggest that if opportunities for spiritual growth are presented, there will be overwhelming interest from most congregations. Here are three methods of promoting spiritual formation in your local church.

Small groups go by various names such as community groups, body life, Bible class, and other names. Small groups have become the place where the most real transformation occurs in churches today. All small groups can and should be catalysts for spiritual development. However, a church may want to have one or more small groups that focus on spiritual formation. Since most small groups rotate through various topics, a church may want to provide the curriculum and leadership and encourage their small groups to use the curriculum for a period of time. There is a lot of material available.[161] Small group leaders should receive specific training in how to assist people in their spiritual journeys. Sometimes this is called a spiritual director, but I prefer the term *spiritual coach*, and there is a lot of information available on how to develop your skills as a spiritual director.

Spiritual retreats are very popular and are held by several organizations, such as the Upper Room Walk to Emmaus.[162] For churches that have the resources, I would encourage you to develop your own material and sponsor your own retreats. A spiritual retreat with a Charismatic emphasis would be a powerful tool for drawing people closer to Christ and helping them discover their spiritual gifts at the same time. A retreat is usually led by a pastor, spiritual coach, or someone who has been on a spiritual retreat led by others. As stated before, I encourage churches to develop their own resources and

The Role of the Charismatic Church

leaders so that they are not dependent on others who may not share their values.

A spiritual coach is similar to an accountability partner. This concept is used in many programs related to personal goals and improvement. Spiritual formation is related to a very special need, and the spiritual coach works one-on-one with a person to help them in their journey. The primary skills of the spiritual coach are to be a good listener and—very importantly—to have a strong sense of spiritual discernment and godly wisdom. The coach does not become the voice of God, but they help the traveler hear and discern the voice of God.

The Church as a House of Prayer

Prayer is the necessary prerequisite for spirituality and, therefore, a prime component of the foundation of a Charismatic church. Prayer and worship create a spiritual atmosphere that allows people to connect with the Holy Spirit. If prayer is neglected, Charismatic activity will soon become formalistic rituals based on human activity rather than the true work of the Spirit. Charismatics sometimes learn to speak the language and imitate spiritual gifts while operating in the flesh. There can be no real spirituality without continuous prayer. When Jim Cymbala's father-in-law talked him into becoming the pastor of Brooklyn Tabernacle, he felt unprepared for the task. The first year, the church did not go well, and Cymbala was unsure if the church would make it. He went away for a prayer sabbatical to hear from God. When he returned, he announced to the congregation:

> From this day on, the prayer meeting will be the barometer of our church. What happens on Tuesday night will be the gauge by which we will judge success or failure because that will be the measure by which God blesses us.[163]

Brooklyn Tabernacle, based on this model, went from being a very small, struggling church to one of the larges Charismatic churches in the nation. They also avoided many of the failures of other Charismatic churches because they placed prayer at the center of their agenda. Many of Cymbala's most inspiring stories related in his books come not from the Sunday worship service, but from the prayer meetings. He writes,

> In the weeks that followed, answers to prayer became noticeable. New people gradually joined, with talents and skills that could help us. Unsaved relatives and total strangers began to show up. We started thinking of ourselves as a Holy Ghost emergency room where people in spiritual trauma could be rescued.[164]

Jesus established the normative standard for the church when he said, "My house shall be called a house of prayer" (Matt. 21:13). Despite Jesus' emphasis on prayer, many question its purpose and effectiveness. The prevailing theology today is that prayer changes the person to be in alignment with God's will but does not move God to action. Some argue that God has already predetermined every event that will happen on earth, including the choices we make.[165] There are many Scriptures, however, that support the theology that what we do and say has an impact on God's response. Nineveh's repentance after the preaching of Jonah is perhaps the clearest example. God sent Jonah to preach to the people of Nineveh that he, God, was about to destroy their city because of their wickedness. After Jonah preached this message to them, everyone, including the king, repented with great sorrow (Jn. 3:6–9). In response to their prayers of repentance, "When God saw what they did and how they turned from their evil ways, he relented and did not bring on them the destruction he had threatened" (Jn. 3:10). Some would argue that their repentance was foreordained by God and thus forced on them, but the text does not support that argument.

Another great example of God's response to prayer is when God had in mind to destroy those in Israel who had turned to idolatry. Moses interceded with God to spare the people:

The Role of the Charismatic Church

> But Moses sought the favor of the Lord his God. "Lord," he said, "why should your anger burn against your people, whom you brought out of Egypt with great power and a mighty hand? Why should the Egyptians say, 'It was with evil intent that he brought them out, to kill them in the mountains and to wipe them off the face of the earth'? Turn from your fierce anger; relent, and do not bring disaster on your people. Remember your servants Abraham, Isaac, and Israel, to whom you swore by your own self: 'I will make your descendants as numerous as the stars in the sky, and I will give your descendants all this land I promised them, and it will be their inheritance forever.'" Then the Lord relented and did not bring on his people the disaster he had threatened. Ex. 31: 11–14

The wording of God's response is the same as the wording used when Nineveh repented of their sins. The Lord "relented" (NIV), the Lord "repented" (King James), the Lord "changed his mind" (NASB 1995). Turning to the New Testament, James writes,

> Elijah was a human being, even as we are. He prayed earnestly that it would not rain, and it did not rain on the land for three and a half years. Again he prayed, and the heavens gave rain, and the earth produced its crops. James 5:17–18

The parable of the persistent widow teaches us that "we should always pray and not give up" (Lk. 18:1–8). Jesus also wrote, "If you remain in me and my words remain in you, ask whatever you wish, and it will be done for you" (Jn. 15:7). Our will can never override God's sovereign will, but if we pray within the bounds of God's will, he has promised to answer the prayer of faith. Rather than believing that God has predetermined every event, Charismatics believe that God makes a range of choices available to us. Within those boundaries, our prayers and faithful actions can make a difference.

When prayer becomes one of the most important elements of the church, it creates an awareness of God's presence and focuses our attention and expectation on God. When prayer is rooted in faith, it is not an empty ritual. God's people should learn to testify of answers to prayer. Prior to the written Scriptures, Israel preserved their history through oral testimonies. Every generation knew how God brought them out of Egypt, parted the waters of the Red Sea, provided for them in the wilderness, and drove their enemies out of Canaan. A Charismatic church should be a house of prayer—a place of community prayer. The Church should also teach and preach about prayer in a way that encourages members to make it a regular part of their individual and family lives. This means that spiritual leaders should model, teach, and testify about the importance of prayer in their own lives.

Praying in Tongues

> For this reason, the one who speaks in a tongue should pray that they may interpret what they say. For if I pray in a tongue, my spirit prays, but my mind is unfruitful. So what shall I do? I will pray with my spirit, but I will also pray with my understanding; I will sing with my spirit, but I will also sing with my understanding. Otherwise, when you are praising God in the Spirit, how can someone else, who is now put in the position of an inquirer, say "Amen" to your thanksgiving, since they do not know what you are saying? You are giving thanks well enough, but no one else is edified. I thank God that I speak in tongues more than all of you. But in the church, I would rather speak five intelligible words to instruct

The Role of the Charismatic Church

> others than ten thousand words in a tongue. 1 Cor. 14:13–19

Paul emphasized the value of praying in tongues, and that fact should never be denied. Although many Charismatics do not speak in tongues, Scripture is clear concerning the value Paul placed on tongues for edifying the believer. Within the public assembly, Paul states that a believer should only speak in tongues if someone is present with the gift of interpretation of tongues; otherwise, "If there is no interpreter, the speaker should keep quiet in the church and speak to himself and to God" (1 Cor. 14:28). When Paul writes, "I thank God that I speak in tongues more than all of you" (1 Cor. 14:18), he most likely is referring to his prayer life as there is no mention of interpreted tongues anywhere except in Corinth. Paul's rationale for prohibiting speaking in tongues in a public assembly is that if a seeker or nonbeliever comes into the meeting, they will be offended. This does not directly address the issue of small group prayer meetings. Non-believers are less likely to come to prayer meetings, and if they do, they are expecting something more than a worship service. Every church should set their own standards concerning the use of tongues in a prayer meeting, but you might consider allowing (or encouraging) speaking in tongues in prayer meetings even if there is no interpretation; this would not violate Paul's intention if the prayer service were otherwise conducted in a manner that is honoring to God and not offensive to those who attend. Too often, believers who do not speak in tongues feel like they are looked down upon for not doing so, and the leaders should make sure this attitude does not become a hindrance to unity. Although praying in tongues should be encouraged, and some Charismatics believe that all believers can speak in tongues, most Charismatics hold that tongues is a gift like any other gift—rejecting the idea that tongues as a prayer language or as a sign of the Baptism is different from the gifts and is available to everyone.

The Church's Role in Spiritual Gifts

> Follow the way of love and eagerly desire gifts of the Spirit, especially prophecy. 1 Cor. 14:1

> Therefore, my brothers and sisters, be eager to prophesy, and do not forbid speaking in tongues. But everything should be done in a fitting and orderly way. 1 Cor. 14:39–40

We discussed how to identify and acquire spiritual gifts in Chapter 3. In this chapter, I want to talk about the role of the church in helping people identify and develop their spiritual gifts. Sam Storms is right that there are many church leaders who say they believe in the gifts of the Spirit, but they are "functional cessationists,"[166] meaning that they don't actively practice the supernatural gifts. Storms understands that unless the church teaches and promotes spiritual gifts, they most likely will not occur to any great extent in the church. Just as Timothy needed to be reminded to stir up his spiritual gift (2 Tim. 1:6), the church has a continual need to encourage people in the identification, understanding, and use of their spiritual gifts.

Spiritual gifts are given to people within the body of Christ—not to individuals who wish to operate on their own as "independent" ministers (1 Cor. 12:28). Gifts can only function in a proper way when they are exercised in the body and under the leadership of the church body. Timothy received certain gifts through the laying on of hands by the elders (1 Tim. 4:14). If the elders of the local church encourage people to pursue their giftings, there is a far greater likelihood that the people will be aware of what God is doing in their life. The shepherd—whether it is an elder or a small group leader—can be more helpful in assisting people in identifying their gifts than a gifts survey. People who feel they have received a revelation (a word from the Lord) should be

The Role of the Charismatic Church

instructed to first share their revelation with an elder or someone else in leadership prior to sharing it publicly. In this way, the person learns how to use their gift for the edification of the body. It is a myth that a revelation overcomes the person, and they are compelled by the Spirit to speak (1 Cor. 14:32). Likewise, a person with the gift of tongues should be taught by the spiritual leaders of the church how and when to use their gift in prayer and, if appropriate, in the public assembly with interpretation.

A word of caution is in order concerning gifts of revelation (prophecy, tongues, interpretation, and dreams). There should be no doubt that God desires to give revelatory messages to his church today. In Joel's prophecy, which Peter referred to on the Day of Pentecost, God said,

> And afterward, I will pour out my Spirit on all people.
> Your sons and daughters will prophesy, your old men
> will dream dreams, your young men will see visions.
> Even on my servants, both men and women, I will
> pour out my Spirit in those days. Joel 2:28–29

Nearly all Charismatics will identify this promise as still relevant today. Paul also told the church at Corinth, "Therefore, my brothers and sisters, be eager to prophesy, and do not forbid speaking in tongues" (1 Cor. 14:29). Why then do we need a word of caution? It is because of the great potential for abuse—intentional or unintentional—from those who believe that they have a revelation from God but are prophesying "delusions of their own minds" (Jer. 14:14). Many times, people are well meaning but their own human will and desires may lead them to be deceived. Nearly every Charismatic church has experienced, at least on some small scale, the effects of someone giving a prophetic message that turned out to be false. Why, then, should we embrace prophecy at all? Why not just agree with the cessationists that God no longer speaks in that way? There are two reasons we cannot go that route. The first is that God gave the prophetic gifts to the church (Acts 2:17–18; 1 Cor. 12–14; Rom. 12:6; Eph. 4:11). The second is that when properly administered, the prophetic gifts are a tremendous source of God's empowerment to the church and, through the church, to the world. The prophetic gifts are a tremendous responsibility and privilege to the church—especially the Charismatic church.

First Corinthians chapters 12 through 14 were written specifically to address how spiritual gifts are to be used in the church. Paul did not chastise the Corinthians because of their use of the gifts, nor did he discourage the use of any gift; he merely gave some guiding principles for the use of the gifts. Paul's overriding concern was that the gifts be used to serve members of the body, not for personal glory, and that everything is done "in a fitting and orderly way" (1 Cor. 14:40).

Promoting Holiness

> Make every effort to live in peace with everyone and to be holy; without holiness, no one will see the Lord.
> Hebrews 12:14

> But just as he who called you is holy, so be holy in all you do; for it is written: "Be holy, because I am holy."
> 1 Pet. 1:15–16

We discussed holiness in more detail in Chapter 7, but here we want to talk about the role of the church in promoting holiness. Holiness is especially important to the Charismatic church because we face unique challenges. Paul addressed 1 Corinthians to "those who are sanctified . . . called to be holy" at Corinth (1 Cor. 1:2). However, he later writes, "And I, brothers and sisters, could not speak to you as spiritual people, but only as fleshly, as to infants in Christ" (1 Cor. 3:1 NASB). He chastises them for their sexual immorality (1 Cor. 5:1, 6:18), for abusing the Holy Communion or Lord's Supper (1 Cor. 11:17–22), and for using spiritual gifts for their own personal gratification (1 Cor. 14: 12–28). As Paul stated in 1 Corinthians 3:1, this was truly a fleshly or

The Role of the Charismatic Church

carnal church, but they were still the "people of God" (1 Cor. 1:2). Spiritual gifts must be used to serve and build up others in the church. Because of the fallen human nature of mankind, there is a tendency to use gifts and talents to call attention to self. Everyone wants to use their spiritual gifts, and they tend to see their gifts as being more important than others'. A person who believes they have a word from the Lord may feel compelled to give out that word at the first opportunity. After all, a word from the Lord is important! Similarly, a person with an urge to speak in tongues may feel that giving that message and awaiting the interpretation is so urgent that everything else must stop while God speaks through them. It is just in this context that Paul writes, "The spirits of prophets are subject to the control of prophets. For God is not a God of disorder but of peace" (1 Cor. 14:32–33). Elders must remain strong, wise, and discerning in how they handle people and their use of gifts in the worship service. The elders should know whether there are people in your congregation with the gift of interpreting messages in tongues. If there are no interpreters in the local congregation, "the speaker [in tongues] should keep quiet in the church and speak to himself and to God" (1 Cor. 14:28). The Spirit does not force or compel a person to speak, whether by prophecy or in tongues, and any urge to speak must be governed by the circumstances. None of us are so spiritually perfect that we can be sure God wants us to exercise a gift at a moment the leadership finds to be inappropriate. Paul tells the Ephesians (and you and I),

> You were taught, with regard to your former way of life, to put off your old self, which is being corrupted by its deceitful desires; to be made new in the attitude of your minds; and to put on the new self, created to be like God in true righteousness and holiness. Eph. 4:22–25

Certainly, holiness is God's work, but our cooperation requires that we "put off the old self" and "put on the new self." The call to holiness is not unique to Charismatics, but to God's people throughout the world, to everyone who identifies as a child of God.

The church must teach and model holiness. This means teaching about the inner transformation that results in holiness of the heart. Spiritual formation doesn't happen automatically; church leaders—both from the pulpit and in small group discussions—should help people in their spiritual growth leading to holiness of heart. The church can help identify habits and lifestyle choices that help and/or hinder spiritual growth toward inner holiness. Just as important as inner holiness, the church can help people recognize the biblical call to outward holiness—by that, I mean moral conduct, language, and appearance. Conservatives sometimes talk about grace in such a way as to imply that our actions, language, and appearance are not important at all. Paul reminds us, "Whatever you do, do it all for the glory of God" (1 Cor. 10:31). The church should avoid being overly legalistic—the Bible is our guide—but we should help people learn what glorifies God and what does not. We have become so influenced by our culture that many people do not know how to think biblically and spiritually, and they are continuously shaped in their thinking by the culture around them. Paul writes, "Don't let the world around you squeeze you into its own mold but let God re-mold your minds from within" (Rom. 12:2, Phillips). Holiness is best learned and developed in community with others and with help from other mature leaders. We are called to be accountable to one another, and that only happens in community with others. Part of the shepherd's role is to guide people in areas where they are least able to help themselves. The shepherd and others in the church should help identify areas that need attention. The enemy of our souls—Satan—deceives us and offers us excuses to cover up our immature and ungodly habits. In every one of Paul's letters to the churches, he admonished them concerning their areas of weakness where correction was needed. Also, in his pastoral letters to Timothy and Titus, he urged them to teach holiness and to help people know what holiness looks like.

The Role of the Charismatic Church

The Church as a Place of Healing

In addition to prophetic gifts (prophecy, tongues, and interpretation), Pentecostals and Charismatics have always emphasized divine healing. Harvey Cox opines that the thing that draws more people to Charismatic and Pentecostal groups is that "they offer healing."[167] Belief and experience in supernatural healing are not limited to Charismatics. Candy Brown finds that in some non-Western countries such as China and Korea, an experience with healing is the most frequent factor leading to salvation.[168] Brown provides documentation from national polls that suggests "70–80 percent of the total U.S. population believes in divine healing."[169] Charismatic churches should—must—emphasize healing, but only as empowered by the authentic power of the Spirit. We should be honest and admit that very few have the gift of healing today. We cannot answer the question "Why?" because God has not revealed the answer. But we should continue to seek and desire the healing gifts as we do the other gifts. Healing can come through three instrumentalities: (1) God answers the prayers of individuals who may or may not have any kind of related spiritual gift; (2) certain people in the body of Christ may have gifts of healing; and (3) the church can be a place of healing where collective faith and practices create a healing atmosphere where the Spirit of God is present, and healings take place.

First, a Charismatic church should encourage and teach concerning all of the spiritual gifts, including healing. God, in his sovereignty, will decide what gifts to give to individuals in the church, but we are told to "earnestly seek the better gifts" (1 Cor. 12:31). Through teaching and encouragement, people will discover their gifts and learn to walk in faith and wisdom in the stewardship of their giftings. The term *gifts of healing* (1 Cor. 12:9) is in the plural, which indicates that such gifts will vary from one person to another. One person may have greater success with certain types of illness than others. John Wimber, the founder of the Vineyard Association of Churches, was known to have great success in healing, and yet Max Turner states that Wimber's success in praying for people with Down's syndrome was only about one in two hundred.[170] This should not detract from the fact that Wimber accomplished apostolic-like feats for the kingdom of God, but we should be honest about the fact that immediate physical healings are rare in our time. It has been my lifelong prayer that God will release a greater portion of his power in and through the body in these last days, but we should refuse to exaggerate. Also, we know that some people have greater success with demonic-based healings than others. One person may have the gift of discerning spirits or prophetic insight that would aid them in the healing, whereas another may have a more commanding presence that can simply speak creative words of healing. Gifts of healing are distinguished from the gift of faith and the gift of miracles, but there are obvious areas of overlap that could bring healing. As the body of believers comes together to heal the sick, they will bring different gifts together for a more holistic ministry to those in need of healing.

Second, a Charismatic church should encourage all people to pray for the sick and should create an atmosphere of expectancy. The King James translates Psalm 22:33, "But thou art holy, O thou that inhabits the praises of Israel." New translators question the validity of the translation, but the meaning remains valid: God is very much present when his people praise him. God has promised to be with us when "two or three gather in my name" (Matt. 18:20). God is omnipresent, but there are times when his presence is more demonstrated than at other times. During worship, prayer, and Holy Communion, people often experience God in extraordinary ways. The church should lead and encourage people to seek God—including for healing—during these moments.

Third, James encourages the church to exercise gifts of healing collectively.

> Is anyone among you in trouble? Let them pray. Is anyone happy? Let them sing songs of praise. Is anyone among you sick? Let them call the elders of

The Role of the Charismatic Church

> the church to pray over them and anoint them with oil in the name of the Lord. And the prayer offered in faith will make the sick person well; the Lord will raise them up. If they have sinned, they will be forgiven. Therefore confess your sins to each other and pray for each other so that you may be healed. The prayer of a righteous person is powerful and effective. Jas. 5:13–16

I see in this passage that the spiritual leaders of the church may collectively exercise certain spiritual gifts even if none of them individually have the gift. That is to say, a church may practice healing as a supernatural work of the Spirit even if no individual in the congregation identifies as having a specific gift of healing. James implies that healing powers may reside in the body collective. A report from the Church of England states that the Church, as the Body of Christ, is commanded to heal the sick.[171] The paper was developed by a lay group with the hopes of encouraging their ministers to place more emphasis on healing. They stressed that all members of the congregation may participate in praying for the sick. The University of Texas Southwestern Medical School offers a course titled Spirituality and Medicine that teaches medical professionals how to talk to patients about the integration of faith and illness.[172] "According to a *Newsweek* poll, 72 percent of Americans say they would welcome a conversation with their physician about faith."[173] The point of presenting this data is to show that the majority of people have some level of faith, or at least interest, in healing through faith and spirituality. If the medical profession recognizes this interest, it seems clear that the church should be the first and most reliable source for healing through spirituality.

Sam Storms presents a model for church-led healing that does not depend on individual giftedness.[174] He uses an "interview" technique in which the person praying begins by asking questions and listening intensely to discern the cause of the problem. Is it purely physical, or are there spiritual and psychological issues involved? Are there root-cause issues that might block effective healing from taking place? Only after these issues are researched do the people who have come to pray actually begin to seek healing. This model is consistent with James 5, where confession is called for in certain circumstances. Some of those in need of healing will be under demonic oppression, and deliverance for them will often require faith and spiritual maturity on a deeper level. The determination that demonism is involved requires discernment and divine revelation. Too often, well-meaning Christians have concluded that a person was "possessed" when, in fact, they were not. The fact that a person's illness does not respond to prayer or to medical treatment is not always an indication of demonism. Deliverance from demonic oppression was a frequent part of Jesus' healing ministry, but he did not rely on symptoms or physical appearance to detect the presence of demons—it was a matter of revelation.

Along with words of encouragement, we must also acknowledge that gifts of healing and related healing ministries have been abused and exaggerated in the past. In the period 1940 to 1970, a significant number of healing evangelists became prominent in the US. Many of them began as legitimate ministers of the gospel, but some of them became enticed by the desire for success and began reporting exaggerated results, and some fell to the attacks of Satan and succumbed to immorality and fraud. We must use wisdom and discernment to separate the false from the true. It is these kinds of issues that have led many people to distance themselves from the practice of divine healing.

Summary

This book is addressed to the Charismatic church and not just to individuals. It is our hope that pastors and spiritual leaders will use the information in developing their own lives and also in leading the church into a deeper and more active life in the Spirit. A Charismatic

The Role of the Charismatic Church

church is an organized gathering of God's people who place a special emphasis on seeking after and participating in the work of the Holy Spirit. The church at Corinth was fully involved in the gifts of the Spirit, and yet they needed instruction on how to bring their gifts together in a way that would honor God and build up the body of Christ. In every church where the gifts are in full operation, there will be temptations—some as direct attacks from Satan and some from human error—that will threaten the unity of the church, but the risks are more than outweighed by the rewards. The number one reason we should be Charismatic is that it is the will of God that we are so. To be Charismatic is not a choice we make to conjure up something based on our emotions. Rather, it is simply a matter of following the Spirit as he leads the church in worship, ministry, and life. The gifts of the Spirit allow each believer and the body, collectively, to participate in God's work.

It is unlikely that individuals will reach their full potential as Spirit-filled believers unless they attend a church that helps them grow and develop in their spirituality. Not all such churches identify as "charismatic," and this is less important than how they actually go about developing people to grow and participate in the body of Christ through their spiritual giftings. The local church should be a nurturing place that helps people discover their gifts and grow in wisdom and spirituality in the use of such gifts.

The presence of the Holy Spirit is more likely to be experienced in the church, in the presence of other Spirit-filled believers, than by individuals in their solitary lives. Jesus promised to be with the people of God in a special way when we gather together, more so than when we are alone. Prayer has more power, and spiritual gifts are more likely to be administered with power and effectiveness within the church and under the guidance of spiritual leaders. This entire book is aimed toward living the Charismatic life in community with others.

Chapter 10
Demons and Spiritual Warfare

> But if it is by the Spirit of God that I drive out demons, then the kingdom of God has come upon you. Matthew 12:28

> Jesus went up on a mountainside and called to him those he wanted, and they came to him. He appointed twelve that they might be with him and that he might send them out to preach and to have authority to drive out demons. Mark 4:13–15

Peter Wagner states that one of the most difficult concepts for the Western mindset to accept is the reality of demons.[175] Rudolph Bultmann, who some regard as one of the most influential theologians of our time, states that demons are a myth, they are ideas the early Christians adapted from pagan cultures, and even if Jesus and the apostles believed in them, we should not hold to these myths today.[176] John Walton, a professor at Wheaton College and formerly at Moody Bible Institute, argues that the biblical writers gained their ideas about demons from cultural sources, and they are based on the common beliefs of their time.[177] Since this book is written for the Charismatic community and we place a high value on the inspiration of Scripture, there is no reason to try to prove the existence of demons other than

Demons and Spiritual Warfare

to say that demonic spirits are a very significant part of the New Testament narrative. We cannot dismiss demons as myths without destroying the credibility of the entire Bible.

The Origin of Satan and Demons

We are first introduced to Satan as the serpent in Genesis 3. The writer of Genesis does not tell us much about the serpent, and we are left to get a fuller description from various other places in Scripture. There are two Old Testament passages that are widely interpreted as references to Satan. Ezekiel 28:11–17 is literally a prophecy to the king of Tyre, but the references about him exceed what any literal application could bear. Just as we recognize that some Old Testament prophecies are Christological in fulfillment, we also recognize Ezekiel was not referring to an ordinary human being.[178]

> [11] The word of the Lord came to me: [12] "Son of man, take up a lament concerning the king of Tyre and say to him: 'This is what the Sovereign Lord says:
>
> "'You were the seal of perfection, full of wisdom and perfect in beauty. [13]. You were in Eden, the garden of God; every precious stone adorned you: carnelian, chrysolite and emerald, topaz, onyx and jasper, lapis lazuli, turquoise and beryl Your settings and mountings were made of gold; on the day you were created they were prepared. [14.] You were anointed as a guardian cherub, for so I ordained you. You were on the holy mount of God; you walked among the fiery stones. [15.] You were blameless in your ways from the day you were created till wickedness was found in you. [16]. Through your widespread trade you were filled with violence, and you sinned. So I drove you in disgrace from the mount of God, and I expelled you, guardian cherub, from among the fiery stones [17]. Your

> heart became proud on account of your beauty and you corrupted your wisdom because of your splendor. So I threw you to the earth; I made a spectacle of you before kings.

The key descriptions include:

He began as a perfect being (v. 12).

He was in the Garden of God (v 13).

He was anointed and ordained as a guardian cherub (v 14).

He was blameless in his ways from the day he was created till wickedness was found in him (v. 15).

He was driven in disgrace from the mount of God (v. 16).

Another Old Testament passage interpreted as a reference to Satan is found in Isaiah.

> How you have fallen from heaven, morning star, son of the dawn! You have been cast down to the earth, you who once laid low the nations! You said in your heart, "I will ascend to the heavens; I will raise my throne above the stars of God; I will sit enthroned on the mount of assembly, on the utmost heights of Mount Zaphon I will ascend above the tops of the clouds; I will make myself like the Most High. Isa. 14:12–15.

While the NIV addresses him as the "morning star," the KJ and NKJV call him out as Lucifer. Literally and historically, the prophecy is addressed to the king of Babylon, but like the king of Tyre in Ezekiel 28, the prophecy extends beyond human references. In both passages, the recipient is referred to as being cast down to earth, which indicates

Demons and Spiritual Warfare

that they previously held a position that gave them access to the heavenly realms. In the Book of Job, we read,

> One day the angels came to present themselves before the Lord, and Satan also came with them. The Lord said to Satan, "Where have you come from?" Satan answered the Lord, "From roaming throughout the earth, going back and forth on it." Job 1:6–7

> On another day, the angels came to present themselves before the Lord, and Satan also came with them to present himself before him. And the Lord said to Satan, "Where have you come from?" Satan answered the Lord, "From roaming throughout the earth, going back and forth on it." Job 2:1–2

There was a time when Satan could go back and forth between heaven and earth. As a former good angel, he retained access to the gatherings of God's angels in heaven. In both Ezekiel and Isaiah, we read that pride was his besetting sin (Ez. 28:17, Isa. 14:13–14). He was not content to serve God as an angel; he wanted to rise above his appointed position and actually challenge God's authority—"I will make myself like the Most High" (Isa. 14:14).

Other names or references to Satan include:

"The devil" (six times in Matthew and Luke and three times in John)
"The tempter" (Matt. 4:3)
"The prince of the power of the air" (Eph. 2:2 RSV)
"The prince of this world" (Jn. 12:31, 14:30)
"The god of this world" (2 Cor. 4:4)
"The spirit who is now at work in those who are disobedient" (Eph. 2:2)
"The old serpent" (Rev. 12:9 KJV, 20:2 KJV)

The origin of the other demons is a bit more complicated. Many biblical scholars hold that demons were once angels, and they participated with Satan in his rebellion. This is based largely on Revelation 12:3–4: "Then another sign appeared in heaven: an enormous red dragon with seven heads and ten horns and seven crowns on its heads. Its tail swept a third of the stars out of the sky and flung them to the earth." There is little doubt that a third of the angels followed Satan in his rebellion and became fallen angels. But what happened to them after their fall is a matter of speculation. We find references to another group of fallen angels in Jude 1:6 and 2 Peter 2:4.

> And the angels who did not keep their positions of authority but abandoned their proper dwelling—these he has kept in darkness, bound with everlasting chains for judgment on the great Day.   Jude 1:6

> God did not spare angels when they sinned but cast them into hell and committed them to chains of gloomy darkness to be kept until the judgment. 2 Pet. 2:4

Now we must face the question of why some fallen angels are held in chains until the time of the end, and others are free to roam the earth and cause havoc among humans. If we assume that the third of the angels who participated in Satan's rebellion are the same ones who are being kept in chains, they could not be the demons who roam the earth. One theory is that demons are human spirits of people who were exceedingly wicked, and after they died, they were allowed to come back to earth and dwell among (or in) other humans. There does not seem to be any biblical support for this view, but Josephus, the first-century historian, refers to this view, and it has carried through the literature down to the present.[179] Proponents of the view that demons are human spirits offer it as an explanation for who the demons are if the fallen angels are currently held in chains.

A better explanation is that offered by Merrill Unger, who argues that there are two groups of fallen spirits.[180] One group is being held in chains while a second is free to roam the earth. Those who rebelled with Satan committed the sin of rebellion as a result of pride. The fallen angels mentioned in Jude and 2 Peter committed a more serious sin and, consequently, are not permitted to roam freely on the earth. Those who are bound could have been part of the one-third who rebelled with Satan, who then committed a more serious sin, or they could be a second group who rebelled in a more serious way. This could explain the response of the demons in Matthew 8:29. "What do you want with us, Son of God?" they shouted. "Have you come here to torture us before the appointed time?" These demons recognized that at some point in the future, they would be sent into confinement or destruction, but they feared that Jesus might send them there prematurely. Only God knows why Satan and his demons are allowed to exist and roam the earth, but that is God's sovereign choice. However, the group held in chains committed such sins that God confined them to chains while allowing others to continue to roam. Unger states they are "too depraved and harmful to be allowed to roam upon the earth."[181]

Kingdoms in Conflict

Spiritual warfare is not just at the individual level—it is primarily a conflict between the kingdom of God and the kingdom of Satan. John the Baptist came to prepare the way for the Lord, crying out, "The time has come. . . . The kingdom of God has come near" (Mk. 1:15). Jesus began his ministry with the same message, "I must proclaim the good news of the kingdom of God to the other towns also, because that is why I was sent" (Lk. 4:43). Jesus sent his disciples out with the same instructions: "to proclaim the kingdom of God and to heal the sick" (Lk. 9:2). The message of the gospel is "the kingdom of God" has come to earth. But with the coming of God's kingdom also came conflict with Satan's kingdom.

> From the days of John the Baptist until now, *the kingdom of heaven has been subjected to violence,* and violent people have been raiding it. Matt. 11:12

> *The god of this age* has blinded the minds of unbelievers, so that they cannot see the light of the gospel that displays the glory of Christ, who is the image of God. 2 Cor. 4:4

> As for you, you were dead in your transgressions and sins, in which you used to live when you followed the ways of this world and of *the ruler of the kingdom of the air*, the spirit who is now at work in those who are disobedient. Eph. 2:1–2

> But if it is by the Spirit of God that I drive out demons, then the kingdom of God has come upon you. Matt. 12:28

The kingdom of God and the kingdom of Satan have been in conflict since Satan's fall, but the level of conflict has increased since Jesus began his ministry. John's proclamation concerning the arrival of the kingdom begins a new epoch in kingdom history. Spiritual warfare is not simply at the individual level; it is kingdom warfare.[182] As with any war, there are gives and takes. The warfare between archangels and high-level demons in Daniel 10 demonstrates that victory is sometimes delayed, and the evil forces sometimes win battles along the way.

There is strong biblical evidence that angels—good and bad—are organized and have ranks and a leadership structure, each with different levels of strength and authority. When the disciples tried to cast out a demon and failed, they asked Jesus why they were not able to cast it out. Jesus first responded that it was their lack of faith, but then he added, "This kind can come out only by prayer [and fasting]" (Mk. 9:29). The word *fasting* is omitted from the NIV due to a textual variant. However, the basic insight, even omitting the fasting clause, informs us that some demons are stronger than others. The text cannot mean they needed to pray more at the moment of the exorcism because Jesus cast it out immediately. The best interpretation is that prayer and fasting prepare the warrior for the moment of battle.

We also know there are archangels who are superior to other angels. The only archangel mentioned by name is Michael (Jude 1:9), and he is also called a "chief prince" (Dan. 10:13). Gabriel is mentioned as having special standing with God, and it is assumed he is also an archangel or one of high authority (Dan. 8:16, 9:21; Lk. 1:19). These angels have assignments, including territorial assignments. In Daniel's encounter with Gabriel, we read:

> Then he continued, "Do not be afraid, Daniel. Since the first day that you set your mind to gain understanding and to humble yourself before your God, your words were heard, and I have come in response to them. But the prince of the Persian kingdom resisted me for twenty-one days. Then Michael, one of the chief princes, came to help me, because I was detained there with the king of Persia. Now I have come to explain to you what will happen to your people in the future, for the vision concerns a time yet to come." Dan. 10:12–14

The passage in Daniel 10 reveals a great deal about the hierarchy and structure of angels and demons. We learn that even angels have to fight spiritual warfare, and victory does not always come easy. Gabriel was dispatched from heaven to bring a message to Daniel. He was intercepted enroute by a strong demon who was assigned to the territory of Persia. In verse 13, he is first called the prince of Persia, and later he is called the king of Persia. The demon is identified by the person or territory to which he is assigned. When Gabriel was unable to break through on his own, the archangel Michael, one of the "chief princes," came to assist him. On his return trip, Gabriel anticipates that he will have to fight the prince of Persia and the prince of Greece, but again, he expects that Michael will help him (Dan. 10:20–21). Also, in verse 21, Michael is identified as "your prince," indicating that Michael has a special relationship with Israel.

In the apocalyptic letter to the church in Pergamum, John was instructed to write, "I know where you live—where Satan has his throne" (Rev. 2:13). Since Satan is a spirit and does not occupy physical space, his throne is the center of his operations. Satan is very intelligent and, therefore, very strategic in the way he goes about his work. In the Parable of the Weeds (or tares), we find that Satan sowed weeds among the wheat (Matt. 13:36–43). This infiltration is by people who look and act like the people of God but they are, in fact, "sons of the evil one," and they are strategically planted in the kingdom of God to cause disruption.

During his earthly ministry, Jesus spoke about the kingdom as both present and future; scholars sometimes refer to this as "yet and not yet," meaning the kingdom had arrived on earth, and yet there was a future aspect yet to be fulfilled. We cannot speak of the beginning of the kingdom of God because Scripture does not tell us when or if there was a beginning point. We can only speak of its arrival on the earth. In one sense, it was already present in the Old Testament, but John's ministry signaled a new epoch in the kingdom, and that included conflict with Satan's kingdom. The present aspect of the kingdom is evident in the teachings of John and Jesus. John said, "Repent, for the kingdom of heaven has come near" (Matt. 3:2). Likewise, Jesus began his ministry with the same message: "Repent, for the kingdom of heaven has come near" (Matt. 4:17). The future aspect of the kingdom is also reflected in the teachings of Jesus. "Then the King will say to those on his right, 'Come, you who are blessed by my Father; take your inheritance, the kingdom prepared for you since the creation of the world" (Matt. 25:34). In the Lord's Prayer, he taught his disciples to pray, "Our Father in heaven, hallowed be your name, your kingdom come, your will be done, on earth as it is in heaven" (Matt. 6:9–10). Peter speaks about the future of the kingdom when he writes, "For if you do these things, you will never stumble, and you will receive a rich welcome into the eternal kingdom of our Lord and Savior Jesus Christ" (2 Pet. 1:10–11). Some of Jesus' sayings could have a double meaning. For example, "For I tell you that unless your righteousness surpasses that of the Pharisees and the teachers of the law, you will certainly not enter the kingdom of heaven" (Matt. 5:20)—this statement is usually interpreted as future, but it could also have present implications.[183]

It is important to understand that spiritual warfare is not only personal and individual, but it is also kingdom against kingdom. As with any warfare, we will win some battles, and we will also lose some battles, but the ultimate victory is guaranteed through Christ. The present kingdom of God is a kingdom in conflict—the war is not over. Daniel's vision describes the war against the people of God:

> As I watched, this horn was waging war against the
> holy people and defeating them, until the Ancient of
> Days came and pronounced judgment in favor of the
> holy people of the Most High, and the time came
> when they possessed the kingdom. Dan. 7:21–22

We can be sure of two things: (1) there will be times when the enemy scores victories against the saints, but (2) God's kingdom will ultimately win. You will suffer disappointment and despair if you expect to win every battle, and nothing will ever harm you. John the Baptist, Jesus, Paul, and Peter were all killed by Satan and his followers. Jesus and Paul had miraculous gifts, but they did not use their gifts to avoid cruel treatment because they knew that God allowed the treatment against them. We have this testimony from the three who went through the fire:

> Shadrach, Meshach, and Abednego replied to him, "King Nebuchadnezzar, we do not need to defend ourselves before you in this matter. If we are thrown into the blazing furnace, the God we serve is able to deliver us from it, and he will deliver us from Your Majesty's hand. But even if he does not, we want you to know, Your Majesty, that we will not serve your gods or worship the image of gold you have set up." Dan. 3:16–17

We must fight to win! In spite of the fact that Satan is still allowed to roam and attack, God has empowered his people to fight and win! While some have argued that miracles such as healing are rare, the promises of God are still true, and his power remains great. When we confront Satan in a power encounter—healing on demon expulsion—Satan knows what power we have (Acts 19:13–16). When Jesus confronted demons, they wilted in fear because they knew his power (Matt. 8:29). We should not simply give up because the enemy is strong; we are called to grow strong in our faith through prayer, fasting, and knowledge of Scripture. When the disciples were not able to cast out a demon, Jesus did not say, "Because Satan is too strong"; rather, he said,

> Because you have so little faith. Truly I tell you, if you have faith as small as a mustard seed, you can say to this mountain, "Move from here to there," and it will move. Nothing will be impossible for you. Matt. 17:20

If we take Jesus at his word, the battles may be long, but faith will eventually produce victory. The statement that we can move mountains is a metaphor meaning there is no limit to what can be achieved through faith.

Demonic Attacks on Believers

Resist the devil, and he will flee from you. Jas. 4:7

Be alert and of sober mind. Your enemy the devil prowls around like a roaring lion looking for someone to devour. 1 Pet. 5:8

Satan and his demons are out on bail and are allowed to roam somewhat freely around the universe until God confines them for eternity. Meanwhile, we will resist them and sometimes do outright battle with them. Resistance does not result in automatic victory or annihilation. Jesus resisted Satan's temptations at the beginning of his ministry (Matt. 4:1–11), but Jesus' victory was not his final encounter with the evil one. The description of the temptation ends with these words: "Then the devil left him, and angels came and attended him" (Matt. 4:11). Many of our spiritual failures occur when Satan takes advantage of our own weaknesses. "When tempted, no one should say, 'God is tempting me.' For God cannot be tempted by evil, nor does he tempt anyone, but each person is tempted when they are dragged away by their own evil desire and enticed" (Jas. 1:13–14). Our daily battles against evil can generally be won through wise and spiritually discerning responses to the temptations and the snares the enemy lays before us. This type of spiritual warfare does not involve demon possession or demon oppression; it is just us making wise decisions because we know the enemy's tactics. If the enemy discovers a weakness in your life or mine, he will exploit that weakness to his advantage.

One of the most debated issues in theology relates to what effect demons can have on Christians. Most conservatives hold the position that a Christian cannot have (or be possessed by) a demon. The term *demon possession* may be too strong in some cases. Storms writes, "The term 'possession' implies ownership, and it is questionable to say that Satan or a demon owns anything."[184] The King James popularized the term *demon possession* as the translation of the Greek term *daimonizomai*, but most lexicons include within the definition "to be under the influence of a demon," with the understanding that the amount of influence can vary. Contemporary literature simply refers to people who are demonized rather than possessed, but we cannot deny that in the majority of cases in the New Testament where the term *daimonizomai* is used, it refers to a demon inhabiting the person. Wayne Grudem agrees with Storms in saying that the term *possessed* creates a misunderstanding and requires a better definition. It does not mean ownership or even complete control. Grudem answers the question of whether a believer can be demon possessed this way:

> If people explain what they mean by "demon-possessed," then an answer can be given depending on the definition. . . . If by "demon-possessed" they mean that a person's will is completely dominated by a demon, so that a person has no power left to choose to do right and obey God, then the answer to whether a Christian could be demon possessed would certainly be no. . . . On the other hand, most Christians would agree that there can be differing degrees of demonic attack or influence in the lives of believers (see Lk. 4:2, 2 Cor. 12:7, Eph. 6:12, Jas. 4:7, 1 Pet. 5:8). A believer can come under demonic attack from time to time in a mild or more strong sense.[185]

The argument that a Christian cannot be demonized is drawn from several arguments that are based on biblical texts, but the texts themselves do not specifically say a Christian cannot be demonized. The argument is based on logic: a demon could not dwell in a Christian at the same time that the Holy Spirit dwells there. Storms devoted a lengthy discussion to the various challenges proposed about Christians being demonized, and he concludes, "The Christian cannot be owned by Satan nor separated from the love of God in Christ. But none of these texts explicitly rules out the possibility of demonization."[186]

Demons and Spiritual Warfare

R. C. Sproul Writes,

> The Scriptures indicate that Satan can oppress us, assault us, tempt us, slander us, and accuse us. But a Christian who is indwelled by the Holy Spirit cannot be possessed by a demon. Where the Spirit of the Lord is, there is liberty (2 Cor. 3:17). If a person indwelled by the Holy Spirit can at the same time be sovereignly controlled by an evil spirit, then our redemption is meaningless.[187]

Note Sproul's assertion that the believer can be oppressed, assaulted, tempted, and slandered—but not indwelt. The first part is serious enough, even if there is no indwelling. Demon "oppression" usually means that a demonic spirit is working from the outside rather than from within, but the result is the same! It could include addiction, anger, depression, and mental illness. Sproul uses the typical logic to deny the possibility of possession. "If a person indwelled by the Holy Spirit can at the same time be *sovereignly controlled by an evil spirit*, then our redemption is meaningless."[188] But does possession mean *sovereign control*, as he asserts? Probably not. Unger finds that some demonized people are set free when they get saved, but some are not immediately set free, and they require deliverance.[189] We know the same thing is true of people with addictions: some are set free immediately, but some require treatment. If a person is demonized prior to conversion and the demon does not depart immediately upon the person's being saved, that does not mean the person is under the sovereign control of the demon.

Many missionaries who have studied Christianity in other countries—especially in Africa and Asia—are convinced, based on their own observations, that Christians can be under demonic attack and require deliverance. Unger writes, "Believers can be hindered, bound, and oppressed by Satan, and even indwelt by one or more demons, who may derange the mind and affect the body."[190] Peter described Jesus' ministry in these terms: "He went about doing good and healing all who were oppressed by the devil" (Acts 10:38 NASB); "He went around doing good and healing all who were under the power of the devil" (NIV). Although the term *possessed* is used in the New Testament (Matt. 4:24, 8:16, 8:28, 8:33, 9:32, etc.), there is no reason to conclude that in every case, the demon was living continuously in the person. The same can be said of the woman with the curvature of the spine who was said to be a "daughter of Abraham," and yet Satan had "bound her" for eighteen years (Lk. 13:10–13). The Scripture does not say whether Jesus cast out a demon; it simply says that he laid hands on her, and immediately she straightened up. The laying on of hands is normally associated with healing, not demon expulsion, but we know that the sickness was caused by a demon. That she was a "daughter of Abraham" indicates that she was in a relationship with God, but prior to Pentecost, we cannot say that she was a "Spirit-filled believer."

Jimmy Draper, former president of the Southern Baptist Convention, writes:

> One crucial question must be considered. Can a Christian be demon-possessed? The answer is an emphatic "NO!" The Holy Spirit indwells the believer, and no demon can expel Him and possess the believer. The believer is a child of God and is held in the hand of the Son, and the Father, for they are One (Jn. 10:28–30).
>
> Believers, however, can give a foothold or a make a place for demonic forces in their lives (Eph. 4:27). This gives liberty for the demons to work chaos and wreak havoc within a life, bringing devastating doubt and confusion into a believer's heart. This explains how some believers can fall into tragic sin and how

> some could even commit suicide. We must not give
> Satan any place in our lives.
>
> Once a person is freed from demonic powers through
> the power of the Gospel and fellowship with Christ, it
> is vital to develop a dynamic spiritual resistance to all
> forms of evil. Consistent Bible study is basic, and
> fellowship in a dynamic church that stands upon the
> Word of God is necessary. We need each other and
> draw strength from each other.[191]

Draper, more explicitly than Sproul, recognizes the harm that demons can do to believers. However, when Draper writes, "Once a person is freed from demonic powers through the power of the Gospel and fellowship with Christ," is he asserting that this freedom happens immediately upon being saved? Is he ready to argue that every newborn Christian is immediately delivered from every demon-caused addiction and illness? Denying that demons can affect believers makes us vulnerable and unprepared to bring healing and deliverance. This writer was conducting a prayer meeting for a person who was very obviously tormented by demonic oppression. When I began to deal with the demonic forces, another Christian in the room spoke out and said, "It cannot be a demon; she is a Christian." If a situation shows all the signs of demonic activity, we should treat it as such, regardless of the status of the person involved.

Most case histories of Christians being demonized include evidence that the demon entered (or attached themselves to) the person through the person's own actions, such as sinful activities or participation in the occult. There are known cases of Christians dabbling in witchcraft, tarot cards, seances, and other similar activities in which they actively sought to communicate with the spirit world. Such activities open the door for demonization. Many African and Asian indigenous religions make frequent use of actions designed to communicate with spirits other than God's Spirit. Even after becoming Christians, they sometimes mix non-Christian practices into their Christian worship. There is also anecdotal evidence that people who surrender to sexual perversions, including pornography, may become demonized, but that is not always the case.

Casting Out Demons

> Jesus called his twelve disciples to him and gave them authority to drive out impure spirits and to heal every disease and sickness. Matt. 10:1

> When Jesus called the Twelve together, he gave them power and authority to drive out all demons and to cure diseases. Lk. 9:1

When Jesus commissioned the twelve to go out on preaching missions, he gave them power and authority. The Greek text makes a distinction between power (*dunamis*) and authority (*exousia*). Matthew's gospel just has authority, but Luke specifies that Jesus gave them power and authority to heal and cast out demons (Matt. 10:10; Lk. 9:1). Although the words *power* and *authority* are sometimes used interchangeably in English, the terms are really quite different. Power implies the ability to do something by force, strength, or creativity. Authority relies on a system of government, rules, or regulations that require adherence. Jesus gave the apostles the authority to cast out demons, recognizing that the spirits would have to recognize the authority. The demons know who has real authority and who does not. When a group of men tried to cast out a demon by saying, "Come out in the name of Jesus whom Paul preaches about," the demon responded, "Jesus I know, and Paul I know about, but who are you?" (Acts 19:15). The demons knew that these men did not have either the power or the authority. Casting out demons is not listed among the gifts of the Spirit in the New Testament, but it is demonstrated as such. Wesley, in a written defense of spiritual gifts, includes "casting our devils" as a spiritual gift or *charismata*. He states;

Demons and Spiritual Warfare

> Hence, we may observe that the chief *charismata* conferred on the apostolical Church were (1) casting out devils; (2) speaking with new tongues; (3) escaping dangers in which otherwise they must have perished; (4) healing the sick; (5) prophecy, foretelling things to come; (6) visions; (7) divine dreams; and (8) discerning of spirits.[192]

Demons have varying levels of strength (Dan. 10:12–14; Matt. 17:21), and Peter Wagner opines that not all Christians have the authority or power to expel every kind of demon.[193] A careful study of all the cases of demon expulsion in the Bible, by Jesus and by others, we do not find any cases in which they prayed for the demon to leave. Rather, they spoke words of faith and commanded the demon(s) to leave. McClung defined exorcism as "the act of expelling evil spirits or demons by adjuration in the name of Jesus Christ and through his power."[194] He offered this definition in rebuttal to non-Christian sources who credit exorcism to "prayer, divination, or magic." Jesus can expel demons with his spoken word because he is God incarnate. The disciples could speak with authority because they were granted authority by Christ. Lest we think that only the Apostles were given this authority, we find that Philip, one of the seven deacons (Acts 6), later became an evangelist and performed mighty deeds. "When the crowds heard Philip and saw the signs he performed, they all paid close attention to what he said. For with shrieks, impure spirits came out of many, and many who were paralyzed, or lame were healed" (Acts 8:6–7).

Following Wesley's assertion that casting out demons is a spiritual gift, we can assume that it follows the pattern of all other spiritual gifts. It is bestowed by the sovereign will of God according to the needs of the church (1 Cor. 12:18). As with all gifts, its stewardship is entrusted to an individual for the good of others and for the kingdom of God. The steward can develop and grow in their knowledge and spiritual wisdom concerning the use of the gift. A person who is led by the Spirit to cast out demons would be wise to work with a more experienced person to grow and develop their gift. McClung states that most Pentecostals would claim that all believers have the authority to cast out demons because of the priesthood of all believers.[195] The problem with this argument is that it assumes that all believers have equal spiritual gifts and equal power. There is no indication that Philip's experience in Samaria (Acts 8:6–7) was normative among the members of the church. Perhaps the potential exists, but such potential is dependent on giftings and development.

Suggestions for Delivering People from Demons

There is a great need for discernment. People often came to Jesus (or were brought to him) for what might appear to be a normal physical ailment, and Jesus healed the person by casting out a demon. Examples include:

Seizures and muteness (Mk. 9:14–29)

Physical deformity (Lk. 13:10–17)

Blindness and muteness (Matt. 12:22–23)

Muteness (Lk. 11:14–16)

Seizures (Matt. 17:14)

This demonstrates that many—but by no means all—illnesses are caused by demons. The only way to know if something is caused by a demon is through spiritual discernment. We would not assert that all cases of blindness are demonic, but only through supernatural discernment could one know that for certain. Malachi Martin describes the exorcism process involving a team of gifted people.[196] Storms advises that someone on the team should have the gift of discernment.[197]

McClung writes, "Like many themes in Pentecostal/Charismatic belief and practice, exorcism has been practiced but not formally

Demons and Spiritual Warfare

theologized."[198] Whether there is a need for a "theology of demonization" is questionable, but too many leaders tend to avoid this area of ministry because they feel ill equipped or fearful of demons, or they are theologically unsure if demons exist.[199] People who claim to have a "deliverance ministry" often carry things to extremes by seeing demons behind every bush. They imply that every sickness or bad habit is caused by a demon. There are no biblical examples of someone called to a full-time ministry of casting out demons or going out hunting for demons. When Jesus came near a demon, quite often the demon would react by crying out or responding in some similar way (Matt. 8:29). The same appears to be true of Philip the evangelist; the demons cried out when Philip came near (Acts 8:7).

To be demonized carries a stigma such that many people are reluctant to acknowledge that the problem could be demonic. We should emphasize that being demonized does not mean the person is spiritually deficient—or more sinful than other Christians. Even if we were to say a demon was attached (externally) or attacking from the outside, many people are still reluctant to acknowledge the problem could be caused by a demon. Part of this is based on the incorrect teaching that a demon cannot harm a Christian. Also, science casts doubt on the existence of nonhuman spirits, so much so that many people simply do not want to address the issue.

Speak the Word with authority in the name of Jesus. There are no magical formulas or incantations that are the key to successful deliverance. Demonic spirits recognize the authority inherent in the name of Jesus and delegated to believers based on our position in Christ. Faith and confidence in Jesus' name and our position in him bring the power to bear upon the situation. Every believer has power equivalent to their faith, but we should also recognize that our gifts play a significant role. Deliverance is not always instantaneous. Most of the cases in Jesus' ministry were instantaneous, but we see two exceptions in the Bible. When the Archangel Gabriel wrestled with the demonic prince, the fight went on for twenty-one days (Dan. 10:12–14). Also, on one occasion, when the disciples of Jesus tried to expel a demon, they were unsuccessful, and Jesus said, "This kind can come out only by prayer [and fasting]" (Mk. 9:29). We have shown previously in this chapter that demons have different levels of authority and power. Some may not leave without a fight.[200]

Teaching and counseling can be helpful, especially with Christians. Neil Anderson is a teacher, author, and counselor; he was formerly chairman of the practical theology department at Talbot School of Theology. Anderson addresses demonology, especially among Christians, from the perspective of teaching and counseling. He finds that Christians can break the bondage of demonic attacks, and they can reject any demons that may indwell or be attached to them by coming to know their identity in Christ. This solution may have longer-term effects than having the demon expelled by another person. Even if a demon is expelled by a person or group of persons, the person who has been delivered still needs follow-up care.[201]

Summary

Demon spirits are mentioned in both the Old Testament and the New Testament. It would be very difficult to believe in the inerrancy of Scripture and yet deny the existence of demons. Scripture describes demons as being servants of Satan who go about assisting him with his mission. The origin of demons is a matter of debate, but many Bible scholars conclude they are the angels who participated in Satan's rebellion (Rev. 12:3–4). We also know from Scripture that they have varying levels of authority and power, and they have specific assignments—that is to say, the demons are organized to strategically carry out their mission.

The most debated area of demonology is related to questions about what harm demons can do to Christian believers. In the worst-case scenarios in Scripture, demons inhabited people and exercised some level of control over their lives, speech, and actions and often caused sickness. There are some Scriptures that indicate Christians are

Demons and Spiritual Warfare

protected—at least to some degree—from demonism. The most persuasive argument is that if the Holy Spirit lives in a person, a demon cannot live in them at the same time. This is an argument based on logic because Scripture does not state this conclusion. What is more important is that demons can harm individuals regardless of whether they are inside or attached outside the person. Peter warns us, "Your enemy the devil prowls around like a roaring lion looking for someone to devour" (1 Pet. 5:8).

Demons cause all kinds of abnormal behavior and sickness. With many of the people Jesus healed, he did so by casting out the demon(s). Only through spiritual discernment can one know if a sickness is caused by a demon or by other factors. Not all sicknesses—physical or mental—are caused by demons. Demons also interfere with people's lives in a variety of ways in addition to sickness. Examples include poverty, addictions, anger, hatred, unforgiveness, and obstructing our work for the kingdom of God (1 Thess. 2:18). When it seems we are being attacked by other people, Paul reminds us "Our struggle is not against flesh and blood, but against the rulers, against the authorities, against the powers of this dark world and against the spiritual forces of evil in the heavenly realms" (Eph. 6:12).

Demons recognize the authority delegated by Jesus to his followers. The twelve apostles were given power and authority to heal the sick and cast out demons (Matt. 10:10; Lk. 9:1). Philip the evangelist was not an apostle, but he cast out many demons (Acts 8:6–7). The normal method by which demons are cast out is by speaking words of authority using the name of Jesus. The demons recognize the power and authority that exists in Jesus' name, but they also know that not everyone has this power. Throughout this book, we recommend that spiritual gifts are meant to be exercised in the church and not as individuals acting alone. Within the church, the spiritual leaders can teach, guide, and develop people in the use of their gifts.

Endnotes

Introduction

[1] Larry Hart, "Spirit Baptism: A Dimensional Charismatic Perspective," in *Perspectives on Spirit Baptism: Five Views,* ed. Chad Owen Brand (Nashville: B&H Publishing, 2004), 118.

Chapter 1

[2] Craig Keener states that in much of North America, *Charismatic* means "Christians who affirm and practice spiritual gifts but are not members of a Pentecostal church." Craig S. Keener, *Spirit Hermeneutics: Reading Scripture in the Light of Pentecost* (Grand Rapids, MI: Eerdmans, 2016), 11–12.

[3] Peter Hocken, "Charismatic Movement," in *Dictionary of Pentecostal and Charismatic Movements*, ed. Stanley M. Burgess and Gary McGee (Grand Rapids, MI: Zondervan, 1988), 130; Mark J. Cartledge, "Charismatic Theology: Approaches and Themes," *Journal of Beliefs and Values* 25 no. 2 (2005), 177–190. DOI: 10.1080/13617670420000251591.

[4] Hocken, "Charismatic Movement," 133.

[5] Larry Hart, "A Charismatic Perspective," in *Perspectives on Spirit Baptism: Five Views,* ed. Chad Owen Brand (Nashville: B&H Publishing, 2004), 105.

[6] Hart, "A Charismatic Perspective," 126.

[7] Candy Gunther Brown, *Global Pentecostal and Charismatic Healing* (Oxford: Oxford University Press, 2011), 13.

Notes & Bibliography

[8] As reported by Eddie L Hyatt, *2000 Years of Charismatic Christianity* (Lake Mary, FL: Charisma House, 2002), 3.

[9] Keith Warrington, *Pentecostal Theology: A Theology of Encounter* (New York and London: T&T Clark, 2008), 12.

[10] Allan Anderson, *An Introduction to Pentecostalism*, 2nd ed. (Cambridge, UK: Cambridge Press, 2014.

[11] Anderson, *An Introduction to Pentecostalism*, 144.

[12] Karl Rahner argues that God designed the human in his own image, and therefore the human being is designed to be in communication with God. Karl Rahner, *Hearer of the Word*, trans. Joseph Donceel (New York: Continuum Publishing, 1994), 45–74; Karl Rahner, *Theological Investigations*, vol. 6, trans. Karl Kruger and Boniface Kruger (New York: Seabury Press, 1974), 78, 79.

[13] This assertion will be rejected by some who follow Calvin's theory of predestination, but even moderate Calvinists acknowledge that while God draws all people to himself, this does not result in universal salvation. The drawing can be accepted or resisted.

[14] Rudolf Bultmann, "Modernity and Faith in Conflict," in *The Making of Modern Theology: Selected Writings*, ed. Roger A. John (San Francisco: Collins, 1987), 256–57.

[15] Kenneth J. Archer, "A Pentecostal Way of Doing Theology: Method and Manner," *International Journal of Systematic Theology* 9, no. 3 (July 2007): 301–306; Russell P. Spittler, "Suggestions for Further Research in Pentecostal Studies," *PNEUMA: The Journal of the Society for Pentecostal Studies* (Fall, 1983): 39–42.

[16] James K. A. Smith, *Thinking in Tongues: Pentecostal Contributions to Christian Philosophy* (Grand Rapids, MI: Eerdmans, 2010), 12.

[17] Keener, *Spirit Hermeneutics: Reading Scripture in the Light of Pentecost* (Grand Rapids, MI: Eerdmans, 2016), 296–303.

[18] Candy Gunther Brown, *Global Pentecostal and Charismatic Healing* (Oxford: Oxford University Press, 2011), 3.

Chapter 2

[19] By the term *classical Pentecostal*, we mean Pentecostalism as it developed in the early part of the twentieth century and remains the primary position held by the Assemblies of God, Church of God (Cleveland, TN), and others. The term is not meant to be negative or pejorative in any way. For the beliefs of the Assemblies of God see "Constitution and Bylaws of the General Council of the Assemblies of God,"

https://ag.org/About/About-the-AG/Constitution-and-Bylaws.

[20] Keith Warrington, *Pentecostal Theology: A Theology of Encounter* (Edinburgh: T&T Clark, 2008), 124.

[21] Frank D Macchia, *Baptized in the Spirit* (Grand Rapids, MI: Zondervan Academic, 2006), 24. Kindle.

[22] Henry Lederle, *Theology with Spirit: The Future of Pentecostal and Charismatic Movements in the 21st Century* (Tulsa, OK: Word and Spirit Press, 2010), 72.

[23] Roger Stronstad, *Spirit Scripture and Theology: A Pentecostal Perspective* (Baguio City, PHL: Asia Pacific Theological Seminary Press, 2018), 11.

[24] Larry Hart, "A Charismatic Perspective," in *Perspectives on Spirit Baptism: Five Views*, ed. Chad Owen Brand (Nashville: B&H Publishing, 2004), 105.

[25] For a lengthy discussion, see I. Howard Marshall, *Acts: Tyndale New Testament Commentaries* (Downers Grove, IL: InterVarsity Press, 2008), 324. Kindle; Grant R. Osborne, *Acts Verse by Verse* (Bellingham, WA: Lexham Press, 2019), 328. Kindle.

Notes & Bibliography

[26] James D. G. Dunn, "Baptism in the Holy Spirit: Yet Once More—Again," *The Journal of Pentecostal Theology* 19 (2010): 34.

[27] F. F. Bruce, "The Spirit in the Letter to the Galatians," in *Essays on Apostolic Themes: Studies in Honor of Howard M. Ervin*, ed. Paul Elbert (Peabody, MA: Hendrickson, 1985), 37.

[28] Peter Hocken, "Charismatic Movement," in *Dictionary of Pentecostal and Charismatic Movements*, eds. Stanley M. Burgess and Gary McGee (Grand Rapids, MI: Zondervan, 1988), 130.

[29] Roger Stronstad, *Spirit Scripture and Theology: A Pentecostal Perspective* (Baguio City, PHL: Asia Pacific Theological Seminary Press, 2018), 11. Kindle.

[30] For a discussion of what Luke means by Spirit baptism and what Paul means, see Roger Stronstad, *The Charismatic Theology of St. Luke: Trajectories from the Old Testament to Luke-Acts* (Grand Rapids, MI: Baker Academic, 2012); also, I. Howard Marshall, *Acts: Tyndale New Testament Commentaries* (Downers Grove, IL: InterVarsity Press, 2008), 22–23.

[31] Walter C. Kaiser, "A Reformed Perspective," in *Perspectives on Spirit Baptism: Five Views*, ed. Chad Owen Brand (Nashville: B&H Publishing, 2004), 36.

[32] Ibid, 37.

[33] Ralph Del Colle, "Spirit Baptism: A Catholic Perspective," in *Perspectives on Spirit Baptism: Five Views*, ed. Chad Owen Brand (Nashville: B&H Publishing, 2004), 241.

[34] Ibid., 241.

[35] Ibid., 244.

[36] Ibid., 246.

[37] Ibid., 259.

[38] Ibid., 261.

[39] Del Colle, "Spirit Baptism: A Catholic Perspective," 262.

[40] Ibid., 263.

[41] Larry Hart, "Spirit Baptism: A Dimensional Charismatic Perspective," in *Perspectives on Spirit Baptism: Five Views*, ed. Chad Owen Brand (Nashville: B&H Publishing, 2004), 118.

[42] Ibid., 124.

[43] J. I. Packer, *Rediscovering Holiness: Know the Fulness of Life with God* (Grand Rapids, MI: Baker Books, 2009), 21.

[44] Cessationism is the belief that supernatural gifts and displays of power through individuals ceased after the death of the last apostle.

[45] John MacArthur, "What Does It Mean to Be Baptized with the Holy Spirit?"

https://www.gty.org/library/bibleqnas-library/QA0030/what-does-it-mean-to-be-baptized-with-the-holy-spirit.

[46] The term *baptized in the Spirit* is often used in teaching literature but it is not found in the Bible. Other terms frequently used to describe Spirit baptism include *Spirit anointing*, a favorite term used by Jack Hayford. John MacArthur states strongly that the term *baptism in the Spirit* always refers to the new birth and *filled with the Spirit* is the proper term for the baptism in power; however, MacArthur's explanation does not clarify the use of *baptism in the Spirit* in Acts 1:4. See MacArthur's commentary on Acts, Chapter 2.

[47] https://www.desiringgod.org/interviews/john-macarthur-and-strange-fire

[48] Hart, "A Charismatic Perspective," 155–56.

[49] Walter A. Bauer, *Greek-English Lexicon of the New Testament and Other Early Christian Literature*, 3rd ed., ed. Frederick W. Danker (Chicago: University of Chicago Press, 2000), 833. (Hereinafter, BDAG).

[50] Gordon D. Fee, *God's Empowering Presence: The Holy Spirit in the Letters of Paul* (Peabody, MA: Hendrickson Publishers, 1995), 24–26.

[51] Ibid., 25.

[52] George E. Ladd. *A Theology of the New Testament* (Grand Rapids, MI: Eerdmans, 1974), 462.

[53] Craig S. Keener, *The Gospel of John: A Commentary*, vol. 1 (Grand Rapids, MI: Baker Academic, 2003), 615.

[54] Ibid.

[55] Leon Morris, *The Gospel According to John*, rev., New International Commentary on the New Testament (Grand Rapids, MI: Eerdmans, 1995), 239.

[56] Ladd, *A Theology of the New Testament*, 463.

[57] Brooke F. Westscott, *The Gospel According to St. John: The Greek Text with Introduction and Notes*, rev. ed., ed. A. Westcott (1908; repr., Grand Rapids, MI: Baker, 1980), 159.

[58] Gordon D. Fee, *God's Empowering Presence: The Holy Spirit in the Letters of Paul* (Peabody, MA: Hendrickson Publishers, 1995), 24–26.

[59] Watchman Nee, *The Release of the Spirit* (Indianapolis: Sure Foundation Publishers, 1965), 20–21.

Chapter 3

[60] Cessationism is the belief that all supernatural gifts ceased at the end of the first century, roughly the time when the last apostle died. B. B. Warfield opined that the supernatural gifts were bestowed at the hands of the apostles, and when the last apostle died, these gifts could no longer be distributed. B. B Warfield, *Counterfeit Miracles*, rev. ed. (1918; repr., Fig Classics: 2012), 3–22. Kindle.

[61] Donald Gee, *Spiritual Gifts in the Work of the Ministry Today* (Springfield, MO: Gospel Publishing House, 1963), 3, 20.

[62] Sam Storms, *Understanding Spiritual Gifts: A Comprehensive Guide* (Grand Rapids, MI: Zondervan Reflective, 2020), 3.

⁶³ Craig Keener, *Gift and Giver: The Holy Spirit for Today* (Grand Rapids, MI: Baker Academic, 2001), 114; J. R. Michaels, "Gifts of the Spirit," in *Dictionary of Pentecostal and Charismatic Movements*, eds. Stanley Burgess and Gary McGee (Grand Rapids, MI, 1989), 332–34.

⁶⁴ Craig Keener, *Gift and Giver*, 114–18.

⁶⁵ Leslie B. Flynn, *19 Gifts of the Spirit* (Wheaton, IL: Victor Books, 1986), 108–15.

⁶⁶ The Cleveland Clinic, "Why Do We Dream?" August 18, 2022. https://health.clevelandclinic.org/why-do-we-dream/#:~:text=Most%20dreaming%20occurs%20during%20REM, and%20the%20forebrain%20generates%20dreams.

Chapter 4

⁶⁷ Wayne Grudem, *Systematic Theology: An Introduction to Biblical Doctrine* (Grand Rapids, MI: Zondervan, 1994).

⁶⁸ Wayne Grudem, ed., *Are Miraculous Gifts for Today? Four Views* (Grand Rapids, MI: Zondervan, 1996).

⁶⁹ Grudem, *Miraculous Gifts*, 15.

⁷⁰ Ibid., 13.

⁷¹ Richard B. Gaffin, Jr., "A Cessationist View," in *Are Miraculous Gifts for Today? Four Views*, ed. Wayne Grudem (Grand Rapids, MI: Zondervan, 1996), 55.

⁷² Many cessationist argue that *teleios* is a neuter noun and therefore cannot refer to Christ. However, *teleios* refers to a condition, and although it is neuter, as a condition, it can apply to any noun regardless of gender.

⁷³ Gaffin, "A Cessationist View," 56.

⁷⁴ B. B. Warfield, *Counterfeit Miracles* (Edinburgh: Banner of Truth Trust, 1973), 21.

Notes & Bibliography

[75] Ibid., 22.

[76] Ibid., 24.

[77] Gaffin, "A Cessationist View," 150.

[78] Robert Rothwell, "What Are the Charismatic Gifts?" https://www.ligonier.org/learn/articles/what-are-charismatic-gifts.

[79] Gaffin, "A Cessationist View," 63.

[80] Robert Saucy, "An Open but Cautious View," in *Are Miraculous Gifts for Today? Four Views*, ed. Wayne Grudem (Grand Rapids, MI: Zondervan, 1996), 100.

[81] John Piper on Spiritual Gifts Today (and Especially Prophecy), September 29, 2010.

https://www.johnpiippo.com/2010/09/john-piper-on-spiritual-gifts-today-and.html.

[82] C. Peter Wagner, *The Third Wave of the Holy Spirit: Encountering the Power of Signs and Wonders Today* (Ann Arbor, MI: Servant Publications, 1988).

[83] Ibid., 15–24.

[84] Ibid., 57.

[85] William P. Menzies and Robert P. Menzies, *Spirit and Power: Foundations of Pentecostal Experience* (Grand Rapids, MI: Zondervan Academic, 2000), 265. Oss finds that most Pentecostals no longer hold to this view. Douglas Oss, "A Pentecostal/Charismatic View," in *Are Miraculous Gifts for Today? Four Views*, ed. Wayne Grudem (Grand Rapids, MI: Zondervan, 1996), 264, n. 43.

[86] Craig S. Keener, *Miracles: The Credibility of the New Testament Accounts*, Vol. 1 (Grand Rapids: Baker Academic, 2011), 359; Augustine, "The City of God", trans. Marcus Dods in *Nicene And Post-Nicene Fathers of The Christian Church*. ed. Philip Schaff. 2nd.

Edition. (Peabody, MA: Hendrickson Publishers 1995); Eddie L. Hyatt, *2000 Years of Charismatic Christianity* (Lake Mary, FL: Charisma House, 2002).

[87] Anthony C. Thiselton, *The First Epistle to the Corinthians*, Thew International Greek Testament Commentary (Grand Rapids, MI: Eerdmans, 2000), 1063–65.

[88] Gaffin, "A Cessationist View," 56.

[89] Norman Geisler, *Signs and Wonders* (Wheaton, IL: Tyndale House, 1988), 133–36. Geisler repeats Warfield's argument that the supernatural gifts were bestowed only through the laying on the hands by an apostle. Warfield and Geisler make theological assumptions based on patterns with only a few data points and then assume that the pattern is normative. Pentecostals have just as many data points to show that speaking in tongues is normative, but neither position has the full support of Scrripture.

[90] René Latourelle, *The Miracles of Jesus and the Theology of Miracles* (New York: Paulist Press, 1988), 297.

[91] Karl H. Rengstorf, "ἀποστέλλω," in *Theological Dictionary of the New Testament*, vol. 1, ed. Gerald Kittle, trans. Geoffrey W. Bromiley (Grand Rapids, MI: Eerdmans, 1974), 398–447.

[30] Walter Schmithals, *The Office of Apostle in the Early Church*, trans. John E. Steely (Nashville and New York: Abingdon Press, 1969), 25; Walter Bauer, *A Greek-English Lexicon of the New Testament and Other Early Christian Literature* (BDAG), 3rd ed., ed. Frederick W. Danker (Chicago: University of Chicago Press, 2000), 122.

[93] Lightfoot says it is "beyond question" that Barnabas was an apostle. J. B. Lightfoot, *The Epistle of St. Paul to the Galatians* (Grand Rapids, MI: Zondervan, 1957), 96. Textual support includes Acts 13:2–3; Acts 14:4, 14; Gal 2:9).

[94] Clinton E. Arnold, *Ephesians: Exegetical Commentary on the New Testament* (Grand Rapids, MI: Zondervan Academic, 2010), 256–57.

[95] Douglas J. Moo, *A Theology of Paul and His Letters: The Gift of the New Realm in Christ* (Grand Rapids, MI: Zondervan Academic, 2021), 286.

[96] Ibid.

[97] Fivefold Ministry Test.

https://fivefoldministry.com/static/learn-about-the-five-fold-ministry.

[98] The Spiritual Gift of Apostle.

https://myspiritualgifts.com/spiritual-gifts/apostolic/

[99] Stefani McDade, "How Could All the Prophets Be Wrong About Trump?" *Christianity Today*, June 21, 2021,

https://www.christianitytoday.com/ct/2021/july-august/trump-prophets-election-jeremiah-johnson-reckoning-charisma.html;

Julia Duin, "For Christian Prophets Who Predicted Donald Trump's Reinstatement in 2021, No Apologies." *Newsweek*, January 4, 2022. https://www.newsweek.com/christian-prophets-who-predicted-donald-trumps-reinstatement-2021-no-apologies-1665157.

[100] Politico, "The Christian Prophets Who Say Trump Is Coming Again."

https://www.politico.com/news/magazine/2021/02/18/how-christian-prophets-give-credence-to-trumps-election-fantasies-469598.

[101] Craig Keener, "Failed Trump Prophecies Offer a Lesson in Humility," Christianity Today.

https://www.christianitytoday.com/ct/2021/january-web-only/trump-prophets-apologize-election-prophecies-humility.html.

Chapter 5

[102] Kenneth E. Hagin, "Faith Brings Results," Kenneth Hagin Ministries.

https://www.rhema.org/index.php?option=com_content&view=article&id=1026:faith-brings-results&catid=46&Itemid=141.

[103] Charles Swindoll, "What about Divine Healing? Part 1."

https://www.facebook.com/watch/live/?ref=watch_permalink&v=621213211774378.

[104] Keith Warrington, *Pentecostal Theology: A Theology of Encounter* (New York: T&T Clark, 2008), 270–71, n. 25.

[105] John Wimber and Kevin Springer, *Power Healing* (New York: Harper One, 1987), 152.

[106] James Beilby and Paul R. Eddy, eds., *The Nature of the Atonement: Four Views* (Downers Grove, IL: IVP Academic, 2006).

[107] Wayne Grudem, *Systematic Theology: An Introduction to Biblical Doctrine* (Grand Rapids, MI: Zondervan, 1994), 568.

[108] Gustaf Aulén and A. G. Herbert, *Christus Victor: An Historical Study of the Three Main Types of the Idea of Atonement* (Eugene, OR: Wipf and Stock, 2003). Kindle.

[109] Ibid., 122.

[110] R.C. Sproul, "The Ransom Theory," Ligonier Ministries, accessed February 2, 2020.

https://www.ligonier.org/learn/devotionals/ransom-theory/.

[111] Swindoll, "What about Divine Healing?"

https://www.facebook.com/watch/live/?ref=watch_permalink&v=621213211774378.

Notes & Bibliography

[112] *The New English Translation* (NET) affirms that the majority of the early Greek manuscripts include the word *fasting* in Mark 9:29 and a lesser number in Matthew 17:21.

[113] David Hume, "On Miracles" reprinted in *In Defense of Miracles: A Comprehensive Case for God's Action in History*, eds. R. Douglas Geivett and Gary R. Habermas (Downers Grove, IL: IVP Academic, 1997), 33.

Chapter 6

[114] Carl F. H. Henry, *God, Revelation, and Authority*, vol. 1, rev. ed. (1976; repr., Wheaton, IL: Crossway Books, 1999), 4954. Kindle. Henry argues that the Spirit helps us apply and obey the Scriptures, but divine assistance is not required to understand the Bible.

[115] William Klein, Craig Blomberg, and Robert Hubbard, *Introduction to Biblical Interpretation*, 3rd ed. (Grand Rapids, MI: Zondervan, 2017), 99.

[116] N. T. Wright, *The New Testament and the People of God*, (Minneapolis: Fortress Press, 1992), 14.

[117] Ibid., 4

[118] Gordon Fee and Douglas K. Stuart, *How to Read the Bible for All Its Worth* (Grand Rapids, MI: Zondervan, 2014).

[119] Raymond E. Brown, "The History and Development of the Theory of a Sensus Plenior," *The Catholic Biblical Quarterly* 15, no. 2 (1953): 141–162. Brown defines *sensus plenior* as a fuller meaning that God assigned to the text and later revealed the same to a human interpreter.

[120] Klein, Blomberg, and Hubbard, *Introduction to Biblical Interpretation*.

[121] Grant R. Osborne, *The Hermeneutical Spiral: A Comprehensive Introduction to Biblical Interpretation* (Downers Grove, IL: IVP Academic, 2010), 333.

[122] Douglas Moo, "The Problem of Sensus Plenoir," in *Hermeneutics, Authority, and Canon*, ed. D. A. Carson and John D. Woodbridge (Eugene, OR: Wipf & Stock Publishers, 2005); Gordon D. Fee and Douglas K. Stuart, *How to Read the Bible for All Its Worth* (Grand Rapids, MI: Zondervan, 2014), 209.

[123] Klein, Blomberg, and Hubbard, *Introduction to Biblical Interpretation*, 255.

[124] Gary Comstock, "Two Types of Narrative Theology," *Journal of the American Academy of Religion*, 55 no. 4 (1987): 687.

[125] Oxford English Dictionary, s.v. "narrative."

[126] John Goldingay, "Biblical Story and the Way it Shapes Our Story," *The Journal for the European Pentecostal Theological Association* 17 (1997): 5.

[127] Hunsinger states that Frei coined the term *postliberal* to describe Barth's theology, and after that, the term became a theological option in its own right. See George Hunsinger, "Postliberal Theology" in *Kevin J. Vanhoozer, The Cambridge Companion to Postmodern Theology*, 45.

[128] George A. Lindbeck, *The Nature of Doctrine: Religion and Theology in a Postliberal Age* (Louisville, KY: Westminster John Knox Press, 1984), 3700. Kindle.

[129] Henry, *God, Revelation, and Authority*, vol. 1, 4954.

[130] Kenneth J. Archer, *A Pentecostal Hermeneutic: Spirit, Scripture, and Community* (Cleveland, TN: CPT Press, 2009), 134–35.

[131] Mark J. Cartledge, "Text-Community-Spirit: The Challenges Posed by Pentecostal Theological Method to Evangelical Theology," in *Spirit and Scripture: Exploring a Pneumatic Hermeneutic*, eds. Kevin L. Spawn and Archie T. Wright (London: Bloomsbury, 2013), 134.

Notes & Bibliography

[132] Kevin J. Vanhoozer, *The Drama of Doctrine: A Canonical Linguistic Approach to Christian Theology* (Louisville, KY: Westminster John Knox, 2005).

[133] Ibid., 57.

[134] Steven Jack Land, *Pentecostal Spirituality: A Passion for the Kingdom* (Cleveland, TN: CPT Press, 2010), 46.

[135] Kevin J. Vanhoozer, "The Reader in New Testament Interpretation," in *Hearing the New Testament: Strategies for Interpretation*, ed. Joel B. Green (Grand Rapids, MI: Eerdmans, 2010), 269.

[136] James Beilby, "Contemporary Religious Epistemology," in *The Enduring Authority of the Christian Scriptures*, ed. D. A. Carson (Grand Rapids, MI: Eerdmans, 2016), 284, 820.

[137] J. I. Packer asserts that the Holy Spirit does not teach us "fresh disclosures of hitherto unknown truths." J. I. Packer, *God Has Spoken* (Wheaton, IL: Crossway, 2021), 149.

Chapter 7

[138] Gordon Fee, *The First Epistle to the Corinthians*, The International Commentary on the New Testament (Grand Rapids, MI: Eerdmans, 1987), 123.

[139] Dallas Willard, *The Spirit of the Disciplines: Understanding How God Changes Lives* (New York: Harper One, 1999); Dallas Willard, *Renovation of the Heart: Putting on the Character of Christ*, 20th anniversary ed. (Colorado Springs: NavPress, 2021).

[140] John Webster, *Holiness* (Grand Rapids, MI: Eerdmans, 2003), 79.

[141] "Meet the "Spiritual but Not Religious," George Barna Research, April 6, 2017.

https://www.barna.com/research/meet-spiritual-not-religious/.

[142] Karl Rahner, *Spirit in the World*, trans. William Dych (New York: Continuum Publishing, 1994), xvi–xvii, 330–70.

[143] Willard, *Renovation of the Heart*.

[144] Ibid., 27.

[145] Don Carson, "How to Read the Bible and Do Theology Well," The Gospel Coalition Blog, September 24, 2015, accessed November 29, 2021,

https://www.thegospelcoalition.org/article/the-bible-and-theology-don-carson-nivzsb/.

[146] Paul Ricoeur, *From Text to Action: Essays in Hermeneutics, II*, trans. Kathleen Blamey and John B. Thompson (Evanston, IL: Northwestern University Press, 2007), 8.

[147] John Webster, *Holiness* (Grand Rapids, MI: Eerdmans, 2003), 79.

[148] Anthony A. Hoekema, "The Reformed Perspective," in *Five Views on Sanctification*, ed. Stanley Gundry (Grand Rapids, MI: Zondervan, 1987), 61–90.

[149] J. I. Packer, *Rediscovering Holiness: Know the Fulness of Life with God* (Grand Rapids, MI: Baker Books, 2009), 21.

[150] Michael Allen, "Sanctification, Perseverance, and Assurance," in *Reformation Theology*, ed. Matthew Barrett (Wheaton, IL: Crossway, 2017), 552–53.

[151] Peter has quoted from Leviticus 11:44a, "I am the Lord your God; consecrate yourselves and be holy, because I am holy."

[152] Packer, *Rediscovering Holiness*.

Notes & Bibliography

[153] Stanley M. Horton, "The Pentecostal Perspective," in *Five Views on Sanctification*, ed. Stanley Gundry (Grand Rapids, MI: Zondervan, 1987), 105–35.

[154] Henry Lederle, *Theology with Spiri: The Future of Pentecostal and Charismatic Movements in the 21st Century* (Tulsa, OK: Word and Spirit Press, 2010), 54–56.

[155] John Wesley, *A Plain Account of Christian Perfection* (1872: repr., Kansas City: Beacon Hill Press, 1966), 35–37.

[156] G.D. Watson, "Others May, You Cannot," Sermon Index.

https://www.sermonindex.net/modules/newbb/viewtopic.php?topic_id=36129&forum=35.

[157] David A. DeSilva, *The Letter to the Galatians*, The New International Commentary on the New Testament (Grand Rapids, MI: Eerdmans, 2018), 481.

[158] Donald Gee, *Spiritual Gifts in the Work of the Ministry Today* (Springfield, MO: Gospel Publishing House, 1963), 3, 20.

[159] Meet the "Spiritual but Not Religious, George Barna Research.

Chapter 9

[160] "Doubt & Faith: Top Reasons People Question Christianity," Barna Research, March 1, 2023.

https://www.barna.com/research/doubt-faith/.

[161] The two most popular books on this topic are Richard J. Foster, *Celebration of Discipline: The Path to Spiritual Growth* (1978; repr., San Francisco: Harper One, 2018) and Dallas Willard, *The Spirit of the Disciplines: Understanding How God Changes Lives* (San Francisco: Harper One, 1988). Also see Renovare.org., https://renovare.org/articles.

[162] Walk to Emmaus.

https://www.upperroom.org/walktoemmaus.

[163] Jim Cymbala, *Fresh Wind, Fresh Fire* (Grand Rapids, MI: Zondervan, 2008), 27.

[164] Ibid.

[165] John Piper, "Prayer and Predestination: A Conversation between Prayerful and Prayerless," Desiring God, February 14, 1996, https://www.desiringgod.org/articles/prayer-and-predestination.

[166] Sam Storms, *Understanding Spiritual Gifts: A Comprehensive Guide* (Grand Rapids, MI: Zondervan Reflective, 2020), xvii.

[167] Harvey Cox, "Forward," in *Global Pentecostal and Charismatic Healing*, ed. Candy Gunther Brown (Oxford: Oxford University Press, 2011), ii. Kindle.

[168] Candy Gunther Brown, *Global Pentecostal and Charismatic Healing* (Oxford: Oxford University Press, 2011), 14.

[169] Ibid., 3.

[170] Max Turner, *The Holy Spirit and Spiritual Gifts*, rev. ed. (Peabody, MA: Hendrickson Publishers, 1996), 325.

[171] "A Time for Healing" is position paper developed by participants in a working group and published by the Archbishops Council for the House of Bishops (London: Church House Publishing, 2000), 17.

[172] Claudia Kalb, "Faith & Healing," *Newsweek*, November 9, 2003. https://www.newsweek.com/faith-healing-133365. Also, George Washington University established the GW Institute for Spirituality and Health in 2001 with similar goals. https://gwish.smhs.gwu.edu/about.

[173] Ibid.

Notes & Bibliography

[174] Sam Storms, *Practicing the Power: Welcoming the Gifts of the Holy Spirit in Your Life* (Grand Rapids, MI: Zondervan, 2017), 73–81.

Chapter 10

[175] C. Peter Wagner, *The Third Wave of the Holy Spirit* (Ann Arbor, MI: Vine Books, 1988), 57.

[176] Rudolf Bultmann, "Demythologizing," in *The Making of Modern Theology: Selected Writings*, ed. Roger A. John (San Francisco: Collins, 1987), 292.

[177] John H. Walton and J. Harvey Walton, *Demons and Spirits in Biblical Theology: Reading the Biblical Text in Its Cultural and Literary Context* (Eugene, OR: Cascade Books, 2019), 30. Kindle.

[178] Paul Wegner asserts that Isaiah 14:12–15 could not be a reference to Satan because to interpret it that way would require "lifting these verses out of their context," but he has no problem saying that Isaiah 7:14 and 9:6 have dual meanings; they were originally addressed to a human king in Isaiah's day, but they also interpreted *Christological* as referring to Christ. The same hermeneutical principle should apply to Isaiah 14 and Ezekiel 28. Paul D. Wegner, *Isaiah*, Tyndale Old Testament Commentaries (Downers Grove, IL: IVP Academic, 2021), 107, 119, 148.

[179] Flavius Josephus, *Wars of the Jews*, trans. William Whiston (Overland Park, KS: Digireads.com, 2010), 7:6:3.

[180] Merrill F. Unger, *Biblical Demonology: A Study of Spiritual Forces at Work Today* (Grand Rapids, MI: Kregel, 1994), 600–700. Kindle.

[181] Merrill F. Unger, *Demons in the World Today* (Wheaton, IL: Tyndale House: 1971), 16.

[182] There is widespread disagreement about the interpretation of Matthew 11:12 and the violence against the kingdom of heaven, especially if we compare Matthew 11:12 with Luke 16:16. The best solution is to allow each text to stand on its own and not force

agreement. If we allow Matthew to speak plainly, it implies that the kingdom has violent acts perpetrated against it. For a detailed discussion see R. T. France, *The Gospel of Matthew*, The New International Commentary on the New Testament (Grand Rapids, MI: Eerdmans Publishing, 2007), 429; David Turner, *Matthew*, Baker Exegetical Commentary on the New Testament (Grand Rapids, MI: Baker Publishing, 2008), 6917–21. Kindle.

[183] Matthew typically uses the term *kingdom of heaven* as synonymous with *kingdom of god*. Most theologians agree that they are synonymous terms, but dispensationalists such as Lewis Sperry Chafer argue that Matthew distinguished between the two terms. The argument in favor of the two being the same is that when comparing the four gospels, the same passage in Mark and Luke will use the term *kingdom of God*, and Matthew will say *kingdom of heaven*. Matthew may be trying to avoid using th name of God or direct reference to God unnecessarily. David L. Turner, *Matthew*, Baker Exegetical Commentary on the New Testament (Grand Rapids, MI: Baker Academic, 2008), 1466. Kindle.

[184] Sam Storms, *Understanding Spiritual Warfare: A Comprehensive Guide* (Grand Rapids, MI: Zondervan, 2021), 152. Kindle.

[185] Wayne Grudem, *System Theology: An Introduction to Biblical Theology* (Grand Rapids, MI: Zondervan, 1994), 424.

[186] Storms, *Understanding Spiritual Warfare*, 177.

[187] R. C. Sproul, "Are We Too Concerned with Demons?" Ligonier Ministries, July 28, 2014.

https://www.ligonier.org/learn/articles/are-we-too-concerned-demons.

[188] Ibid.

[189] Unger, *Demons in the World Today*, 185.

[190] Ibid., 185.

[191] Jimmy Draper, "DOCTRINE: Demonic Deliverance," Baptist Press, April 19, 2007.

https://www.baptistpress.com/resource-library/news/doctrine-demonic-deliverance/.

[192] John Wesley, "Letter to Dr. Conyers Middleton, London, January 4, 1749," *The Letters of John Wesley*, vol. 2. Wesley Center Online.

http://wesley.nnu.edu/john-wesley/the-letters-of-john-wesley/wesleys-letters-1749/.

[193] C. Peter Wagner, *Engaging the Enemy: How to Fight and Defeat Territorial Spirits* (Ventura: Regal Books, 1991), 25.

[194] M. G. McClung, Jr., "Exorcism" in *Dictionary of Pentecostal and Charismatic Movements*, eds. Stanley M. Burgess and Gary B. McGee (Grand Rapids, MI: Zondervan, 1988), 290.

[195] Ibid. 291.

[196] Malachi Martin, *Hostage to the Devil: The Possession and Exorcism of Five Living Americans* (New York: Harper One, 1992).

[197] Storms, *Practicing the Power*, 169.

[198] Ibid.

[199] Sam Storms, *Practicing the Power* (Grand Rapids, MI: Zondervan, 2017), 148.

[200] Martin details five actual cases of deliverance that were multiday events in *Hostage to the Devil*.

[201] Recommended books by Neil T. Anderson include *The Bondage Breaker* (Eugene, OR: Harvest House, 2019) and *Victory Over the Darkness* (Grand Rapids, MI: Bethany House, 2020).

Bibliography

Allen, Michael. "Sanctification, Perseverance, and Assurance." In *Reformation Theology*, ed. Matthew Barrett. Wheaton, IL: Crossway, 2017.

Anderson, Allan. *To the Ends of the Earth: Pentecostals and the Transformation of World Christianity*. Oxford: Oxford University Press, 2013.

———. *An Introduction to Pentecostalism*, 2nd ed. Cambridge: Cambridge Press, 2014.

Archer, Kenneth J. "A Pentecostal Way of Doing Theology: Method and Manner." *International Journal of Systematic Theology* 9, no. 3 (July 2007): 301–06.

———. *A Pentecostal Hermeneutic: Spirit, Scripture, and Community*. Cleveland, TN: CPT Press, 2009.

Arnold, Clinton E. *Ephesians: Exegetical Commentary on the New Testament*. Grand Rapids, MI: Zondervan Academic, 2010.

Aulen, Gustaf and A. G. Herbert. *Christus Victor: An Historical Study of the Three Main Types of the*

Idea of Atonement. Eugene, OR: Wipf and Stock, 2003.

Barth, Karl. *Evangelical Theology: An Introduction.* Translated by Grover Foley. Grand Rapids, MI: Eerdmans, 1963.

Bauer, Walter. A *Greek-English Lexicon of the New Testament and Other Early Christian Literature,* 3rd ed. Edited by Frederick W. Danker. Chicago: University of Chicago Press, 2000.

Beilby, James and Paul R. Eddy, eds. *The Nature of the Atonement: Four Views.* Downers Grove, IL: IVP Academic, 2006.

Brand, Chad Owen, ed. *Perspectives on Spirit Baptism: Five Views.* Nashville: B&H Publishing, 2004.

Brown, Candy Gunther. *Global Pentecostal and Charismatic Healing.* Oxford: Oxford University Press, 2011.

Brown, Raymond E. "The History and Development of the Theory of a Sensus Plenior." *The Catholic Biblical Quarterly* 15, no. 2 (1953): 141–62.

Bruce, F. F. "The Spirit in the Letter to the Galatians." In *Essays on Apostolic Themes: Studies in Honor of Howard M. Ervin.* Edited by Paul Elbert. Peabody, MA: Hendrickson, 1985.

Bultmann, Rudolf. "Modernity and Faith in Conflict." In *The Making of Modern Theology: Selected Writings,* Edited by Roger A. John. San Francisco: Collins, 1987.

Burgess, Stanley and Gary McGee, eds. *Dictionary of Pentecostal and Charismatic Movements*. Grand Rapids, MI: Zondervan, 1988.

Carson, D. A., ed. *Enduring Authority of the Christian Scriptures*. Grand Rapids, MI: Eerdmans, 2016.

Carson, D. A. and John D. Woodbridge, eds. *Hermeneutics, Authority, and Canon*. Eugene, OR: Wipf & Stock Publishers, 2005.

Cartledge, Mark J. "Charismatic Theology: Approaches and Themes." *Journal of Beliefs and Values*, 25 no. 2 (2005), 177–90.

Comstock, Gary. "Two Types of Narrative Theology." *Journal of the American Academy of Religion*, 55 no. 4 (1987): 687–717.

Cymbala, Jim. *Fresh Wind, Fresh Fire*. Grand Rapids, MI: Zondervan, 2008.

DeSilva, David A. *The Letter to the Galatians*. The New International Commentary on the New Testament. Grand Rapids, MI: Eerdmans, 2018.

Draper, Jimmy. *DOCTRINE: Demonic Deliverance*. Baptist Press, April 19, 2007. https://www.baptistpress.com/resource-library/news/doctrine-demonic-deliverance/.

Dunn, James D. G. "Baptism in the Holy Spirit: Yet Once More—Again." *The Journal of Pentecostal Theology* 19 (2010): 32–43.

Fee, Gordon D. *The First Epistle to the Corinthians*. The International Commentary on the New Testament. (Grand Rapids, MI: Eerdmans, 1987), 123.

———. *God's Empowering Presence: The Holy Spirit in the Letters of Paul*. Peabody, MA: Hendrickson Publishers, 1995.

Fee, Gordon, and Douglas K. Stuart. *How to Read the Bible for All Its Worth*. Grand Rapids, MI: Zondervan, 2014.

Flynn, Leslie B. *19 Gifts of the Spirit*. Wheaton, IL: Victor Books, 1986.

Frei, Hans W. "Response to 'Narrative Theology: An Evangelical Appraisal.'" *Trinity Journal* 9 (Spring 1987): 21–24.

———. *Types of Christian Theology*. New Haven, CT: Yale University Press, 1992.

———. *Theology and Narrative, Selected Essays*. Edited by George Hunsinger and William C. Placher. Oxford and New York: Oxford University Press, 1993.

Gee, Donald. *Spiritual Gifts in the Work of the Ministry Today*. Springfield, MO: Gospel Publishing House, 1963.

Geisler, Norman. *Signs and Wonders*. Wheaton, IL: Tyndale House, 1988.

Goldingay, John. "Biblical Story and the Way it Shapes Our Story." *The Journal for the European Pentecostal Theological Association* 17 (1997): 5–15.

Green, Joel B., ed. *Hearing the New Testament: Strategies for Interpretation*. Grand Rapids, MI: Eerdmans, 2010.

Grudem, Wayne. *Systematic Theology: An Introduction to Biblical Doctrine*. Grand Rapids, MI: Zondervan, 1994.

Grudem, Wayne, ed. *Are Miraculous Gifts for Today? Four Views*. Grand Rapids, MI: Zondervan, 1996.

Gundry, Stanley, ed. *Five Views on Sanctification*. Grand Rapids, MI: Zondervan, 1987.

Gundry, Stanley N. and Gary T. Meadors, eds. *Moving Beyond the Bible to Theology: Four Views*. Grand Rapids, MI: Zondervan, 2009.

Henry, Carl F. H. "Narrative Theology: An Evangelical Appraisal." *Trinity Journal* 9 (Spring 1987): 3–19.

———. *God, Revelation, and Authority*, vol. 1. Wheaton, IL: Crossway Books, 1999. Kindle.

Hodge, Charles. *Systematic Theology*, vol. 1. Grand Rapids, MI: Eerdmans, 1989.

Hollenweger, Walter J. *The Pentecostals*. Peabody, MA: Hendrickson Publishers, 1972.

Hume, David. "On Miracles." In *In Defense of Miracles: A Comprehensive Case for God's Action in History*. Edited by R. Douglas Geivett and Gary R. Habermas. Downers Grove, IL: IVP Academic, 1997.

Hyatt, Eddie L. *2000 Years of Charismatic Christianity*. Lake Mary, FL: Charisma House, 2002.

Keener, Craig. *Gift and Giver: The Holy Spirit for Today*. Grand Rapids, MI: Baker Academic, 2001.

———. *The Gospel of John A Commentary*, vol. 1. Grand Rapids, MI: Baker Academic, 2003.

———. *Spirit Hermeneutics: Reading Scripture in the Light of Pentecost*. Grand Rapids, MI: Eerdmans, 2016.

Kittle, Gerald, ed. *Theological Dictionary of the New Testament*, vol. 1. Translated by Geoffrey W. Bromiley. Grand Rapids, MI: Eerdmans, 1974.

Klein, William, Craig Blomberg, and Robert Hubbard. *Introduction to Biblical Interpretation*, 3rd ed. Grand Rapids, MI: Zondervan, 2017.

Ladd, George E. *A Theology of the New Testament*. Grand Rapids, MI: Eerdmans, 1974.

Land, Steven Jack. *Pentecostal Spirituality: A Passion for the Kingdom*. Cleveland, TN: CPT Press, 2010.

Latourelle, René. *The Miracles of Jesus and the Theology of Miracles*. New York: Paulist Press, 1988.

Lederle, Henry. *Theology with Spirit: The Future of Pentecostal and Charismatic Movements in the 21st Century*. Tulsa, OK: Word and Spirit Press, 2010.

Lightfoot, J. B. *The Epistle of St. Paul to the Galatians*. Grand Rapids, MI: Zondervan, 1957.

Lindbeck, George A. *The Nature of Doctrine: Religion and Theology in a Postliberal Age*. Louisville, KY: Westminster John Knox Press, 1984. Kindle.

Macchia, Frank D. *Baptized in the Spirit*. Grand Rapids, MI: Zondervan Academic, 2006. Kindle.

Marshall, I. Howard. *Acts: Tyndale New Testament Commentaries*. Downers Grove, IL: InterVarsity Press, 2008). Kindle.

Martin, Malachi. Hostage to the Devil The Possession and Exorcism of Five Living Americans. New York: Harper One, 1992.

Menzies William P. and Robert P. Menzies. *Spirit and Power: Foundations of Pentecostal Experience*. Grand Rapids, MI: Zondervan Academic, 2000.

Moo, Douglas J. *A Theology of Paul and His Letters: The Gift of the New Realm in Christ*. Grand Rapids, MI: Zondervan Academic, 2021.

Morris, Leon. *The Gospel According to John*, rev. ed. New International Commentary on the New Testament. Grand Rapids, MI: Eerdmans, 1995.

Nee, Watchman. *The Release of the Spirit*. Indianapolis, IN: Sure Foundation Publishers, 1965.

Osborne, Grant R. *The Hermeneutical Spiral: A Comprehensive Introduction to Biblical Interpretation*. Downers Grove, IL: IVP Academic, 2010.

Osborne, Grant R. *Acts Verse by Verse*. Bellingham, WA: Lexham Press, 2019. Kindle.

Packer, J. I. *Rediscovering Holiness: Know the Fullness of Life with God*. Grand Rapids, MI: Baker Books, 2009.

———. *God Has Spoken*. Wheaton, IL: Crossway, 2021.

Rahner, Karl. *Theological Investigations*, vol. 6. Translated by Karl Kruger and Boniface Kruger. New York: Seabury Press, 1974.

———. *Hearer of the Word*. Translated by Joseph Donceel. New York: Continuum Publishing, 1994.

Ricoeur, Paul. *From Text to Action: Essays in Hermeneutics, II*. Translated by Kathleen Blamey and John B. Thompson. Evanston, IL: Northwestern University Press, 2007.

Schmithals, Walter. *The Office of Apostle in the Early Church*. Translated by John E. Steely. Nashville and New York: Abingdon Press, 1969.

Smith, James K. A. *Thinking in Tongues: Pentecostal Contributions to Christian Philosophy*. Grand Rapids, IL: Eerdmans, 2010.

Spawn, Kevin L., and Archie T. Wright, eds. *Spirit and Scripture: Exploring a Pneumatic Hermeneutic*. London: Bloomsbury, 2013.

Spittler, Russell P. "Suggestions for Further Research in Pentecostal Studies." *PNEUMA: The Journal of the Society for Pentecostal Studies* (Fall, 1983): 39–42.

Storms, Sam. *Practicing the Power: Welcoming the Gifts of the Holy Spirit in Your Life*. Grand Rapids, IL: Zondervan, 2017.

———. *Understanding Spiritual Warfare: A Comprehensive Guide*. Grand Rapids, MI: Zondervan, 2021. Kindle.

Stronstad, Roger. *Spirit, Scripture and Theology: A Pentecostal Perspective*. Baguio City, PHL: Asia Pacific Theological Seminary Press, 2018.

Thiselton, Anthony C. *The First Epistle to the Corinthians*. The International Greek Testament Commentary. Grand Rapids, MI: Eerdmans, 2000.

Turner, David L. *Matthew. Baker Exegetical Commentary on the New Testament*. Grand Rapids, MA: Baker Academic, 2008. Kindle.

Turner, Max. *The Holy Spirit and spiritual Gifts*, rev. ed. Peabody, MA: Hendrickson Publishers, 1996.

Unger, Merrill F. *Demons in the World Today*. Wheaton, IL: Tyndale House: 1971.

———. *Biblical Demonology: A Study of Spiritual Forces at Work Today*. Grand Rapids, MI: Kregel, 1994. Kindle.

Vanhoozer, Kevin J. *The Drama of Doctrine: A Canonical Linguistic Approach to Christian Theology*. Louisville, KY: Westminster John Knox, 2005.

Wagner, C. Peter. *The Third Wave of the Holy Spirit: Encountering the Power of Signs and Wonders Today*. Ann Arbor, MI: Servant Publications, 1988.

_____. *Engaging the Enemy: How to Fight and Defeat Territorial Spirits*. Ventura: Regal Books, 1991.

Walton, John H., and J. Harvey Walton. *Demons and Spirits in Biblical Theology: Reading the Biblical Text in Its Cultural and Literary Context*. Eugene, OR: Cascade Books, 2019. Kindle.

Warfield, B. B. *Counterfeit Miracles*. Edinburgh: Banner of Truth Trust, 1983.

Warrington, Keith. *Pentecostal Theology: A Theology of Encounter*. New York: T&T Clark, 2008.

Webster, John. *Holiness*. Grand Rapids, MI: Eerdmans, 2003.

Wegner, Paul D. *Isaiah*. Tyndale Old Testament Commentaries. Downers Grove, IL: IVP Academic, 2021.

Wesley, John. *A Plain Account of Christian Perfection*. 1872. Reprinted. Kansas City: Beacon Hill Press, 1966.

Westscott, Brooke F. *The Gospel According to St. John: The Greek Text with Introduction and Notes*. Edited by A. Westcott. 1908. Reprinted. Grand Rapids, MI: Baker, 1980.

Wilken, Robert Louis. *The Spirit of Early Christian Thought: Seeking the Face of God*. New Haven, CT: Yale University Press, 2005.

Willard, Dallas. *The Spirit of the Disciplines: Understanding How God Changes Lives*. New York: Harper One, 1999.

———. *Renovation of the Heart: Putting on the Character of Christ*, 20th anniversary ed. Colorado Springs: NavPress, 2021.

Wimber, John, and Kevin Springer. *Power Healing*. New York: Harper One, 1987.

Wright, N. T. *The New Testament and the People of God*. Minneapolis: Fortress Press, 1992.

www.ingramcontent.com/pod-product-compliance
Lightning Source LLC
Chambersburg PA
CBHW050734010526
44107CB00010B/847